Turkish cooking

IRFAN ORGA

Foreword by **Jennifer Paterson**
Introduction by **Ates Orga**

ANDRE DEUTSCH

First published in Great Britain in 1958 by André Deutsch Ltd

This edition first published in 1999 by André Deutsch Ltd
76 Dean Street
London W1V 5HA

www.vci.co.uk

Printed and bound in Great Britain by St Edmundsbury Press, Suffolk

A catalogue record for this book is available from the British Library

ISBN 0 233 99631 1

Design by Kee Scott Associates

Photographs from The Turkish Tourist Board
Capital Pictures

Contents

Turkish cooking

Foreword

Turkish, together with Italian and Chinese cuisine, is one of the three most influential cuisines in the world. China guided the whole of the Far East, Italy taught the French, and Turkey the East Mediterraneans. I am delighted that this excellent book is being re-printed as there are not many Turkish cook books around.

Irfan Orga starts off with a splendid preface on the nature of the Turkish diet. He marvels at the extravagant choice of the ingredients used by individuals in a country with low wages. Many of the receipts are regarded as sacred and have been handed down through the ages so must never be changed in the slightest way. The food is bought fresh every day and immense care and love is put into its preparation. You could say that the Turks live to eat and by chance they have produced the perfect diet so beloved by all the nanny doctors who try to govern our eating habits. Anyone who has lived or eaten in Turkey knows how much better the food is there than in Greece, which is curious as the histories of the two countries are so intermingled.

Cheese is used in many of the fish dishes and I was interested to see the use of bitter almonds in the almond soup (albeit only six as they can produce illness if eaten in any quantity – rather like a cyanide). All the herbs needed for the various dishes are listed and they are wholly available in this country. The chapters on all the very different kebabs and köfte are most enlightening. One very good point about making kebabs is made. You should never thread meat and bits of vegetable on the same skewer as the juices from the onions, tomatoes or mushrooms will toughen the meat whilst cooking. When you think back on it, it's only too true. Turkey (the bird) is boiled first, then stuffed, then roasted, which is probably a very good way of keeping it moist. The vegetable dishes will be invaluable to all as well as to vegetarians and I especially admire the cold ones. There are many delicious puddings – even one made with shredded chicken which I believe, was the original blanc-mange. I very much like the idea of pure lemon jelly – unsweetened, I think it would be a treat with cold salmon. The book is a treasury of good things all handed down by devoted cooks who really care about food. Try them out and make your own Turkish delight!

Turkish cooking

Introduction to 1999 Edition

To my father (1908-70), food was the focus of family life. He had an infectious passion for it. In his memoirs *Portrait of a Turkish Family* (1950), there are vignettes you can almost eat, so vibrant is their recall, so succulent their imagery. Of a circumcision breakfast he wrote, 'the customary white cheese, grapes, boiled eggs and bread and butter, wild cherry and rose jams and tea, served in small glasses with slices of lemon.' Of stuffing vine leaves he remembered their making by Hacer, the old fat cook of dancing buttocks and merry unconfined breasts, supervised by his autocratic, interfering, Macedonian grandmother. Syrup-soaked doughnuts – Kadingöbegi – were as 'light as air and heaven to eat', Lokumlar was of myriad flavour, and there was 'crescent-shaped, pistachio-studded bread' (simit). For lunch by the shores of the Bosphor 'there were roast fowls piled on a mountain of pilaf [pilâv] – rice cooked in butter and chicken-water; swordfish straight from the sea and served with parsley, slices of lemon and various kinds of salads. There were dishes of grapes, watermelons and some kind of heavy sweet made of shredded wheat, butter, syrup and chopped nuts (kadayif). Wine was served in carafes... After the meal Turkish coffee was served under the lime-trees and my elders seemed drowsy, lying back in their chaise longues, their eyes half-shut against the glare of the sun on the grass.' That an archduke had been murdered in Sarajevo, that Europe was locked in empire destruction, that the calling drums of battle would soon be echoing around the wooden-housed streets off the Golden Horn seem hardly then to have mattered. 'War or no war, food must still be served, wine decanted.' As a little boy, 'continually directed to do this, that and the other — all the dirtiest jobs,' my father would be allowed into the kitchens to watch the servants, to be given sweetmeats on the sly, to see how things ought to be done. Like those 'quaint old Turkish songs which made the heart shiver with melancholy,' traditional cookery, he learnt young, was about lovingly-tried rituals handed down by word-of-mouth.

Air-force diplomat turned refugee, Irfan Orga's cooking subtly alchemized the culinary inheritance of a monarchist Ottoman upbringing with a republican Turkish youth. In the English farewell of his life he tamed the wilderness of a Sussex garden to grow grapes. Come late summer mornings he would collect the scented dew-washed pink petals of old-fashioned cottage ramblers to make pots of sugary rose jam, diaphanously veined. In the spirit of the meals he enjoyed creating — culture-reminding 'old family favourites' of unforgettably lavish sight and smell, each a nostalgic excuse for long nights of coffee-and-tobacco aftermath, of reminiscences and stories — his cookery books, informed with social custom and history, imbued with the tastes and textures of an exotic past, were autobiography incarnate. Three appeared in print: *Cooking with Yogurt* (1956), *Turkish Cooking* (1958), *Cooking the Middle East Way* (1962).

At a time when Turkish produce was difficult to find, Turkish restaurants scarcely existed and the kebab take-away was unheard of, *Turkish Cooking* was the first Western attempt to popularize Turkish food and put it on the twentieth century map.

Ates Orga
Suffolk
January 1999

Herbs and Spices

The judicious use of herbs and spices is most important in the intelligent preparation of food, since well cooked dishes will be improved and dull dishes enriched with a subtle flavour. It has been said that the Turks use too much garlic in their food, as well as too much of almost every kind of herb, but this sort of accusation must always be suspect since all nations evolve their dishes to suit their own palate. Any of the recipes in this book can dispense with garlic but, in a Turk's opinion, much of the flavour will have been lost so I would say to anyone who tries these recipes: leave at least an *aroma* of garlic floating around the dish!

Herbs should, if possible, be garden fresh, but if dried herbs are used they should be kept airtight. I am giving a list of the most important herbs used in Turkish cooker and a few general ideals of how to use them.

Allspice (Baharat)

Sparingly in some desserts, fish dishes and meats.

Anise (Anason)

Use the young leaves in salads and the seeds for breads or white cheeses.

Basil (Feslegen)

An excellent and distinctive herb for all salad dishes, white cheeses, beef, veal, fish and sauces. A corrective of rich, fatty dishes.

Bay Leaf (Defne Yapragi)

The leaves should be used sparingly in soups, meats, fish and poultry dishes.

Caraway Seeds (Kimyon)

The seeds give a delicious flavour when grilled with meats and are very good mixed with soft, white cheese.

Chervil (Baharat)

One of the best of all salad herbs. Also good with egg dishes, soups, white cheese, poultry and fish.

Chives (Yaban Sarumsagi)

Gives a subtle and delicate onion flavour and is indispensable with new potatoes, omelettes and white cheese. Also good with fish and certain sauces.

Turkish cooking

Cinnamon (Tarcin)
Excellent in cold dolma stuffing and with braised meats.

Coriander Seed (Cereotu)
Delicate aroma and excellent in stews.

Dill (Tereotu)
Good with lamb, fish, nearly all soups, salads and vegetable dishes served hot.

Fennel (Dereotu)
To be used with fish.

Garlic (Sarumsag)
A herb with a history of 5,000 years. Pungent and stimulating. Can be used in some meat dishes and cold vegetable dishes and with yogurt.

Mace (Kavassyi)
For soups and, sparingly, in stocks. Distinctive flavour.

Marjoram, Sweet (Amarak)
For sauces, soups, salads, beef, lamb, fish, poultry.

Mint (Nane)
Excellent with new peas and new potatoes, salad dressings and lamb and many soup dishes as garnish.

Oregano (Yabani Amarak)
Excellent with lamb and for stuffings

Nutmeg (Zencefil)
Grated in soups and in some sauces and cakes.

Parsley (Maydanoz)
Soups, fish, eggs, meat dishes.

Poppy Seed (Hashas Tohumu)

Excellent with white cheeses, breads and stews.

Rosemary (Biberine)

Gives subtlety and distinction to beef, lamb, veal, sauces and vegetables.

Saffron (Safron)

Indispensable in some kofte dishes and with pilav.

Sage (Ada Çayi)

Fresh sage is far more satisfactory than the dried variety. As the flavour is very evident, the leaves should be used sparingly with white cheeses, some fish dishes, beans, duck, veal and poultry.

Savory, Summer (Baharat)

Leaves and flowers give a distinctive flavour to poultry, beef, lamb, veal, salads and some pilav dishes.

Savory, Winter (Kis Baharat)

Has a very mild and delicate flavour and is excellent with fish.

Sorrel (Kuzu Kulagi)

Delicious with certain vegetable dishes and salads.

Tarragon (Tarhun)

The crumbled leaves should be used sparingly in salads, soups, fish, dressings, veal and poultry.

Thyme (Kekik)

This popular herb enriches and glorifies all thick soups, sauces, white cheeses, beef, veal, poultry and fish and some salad dressings and is particularly good with grilled chops.

Turkish cooking

Preface

During the preparation of this book of recipes I came across some facts which I had not previously taken much note of.

In the first place it was evident how extravagant the Turks are with regard to the raw materials of cookery. Butter, eggs, cream, cheese, oil, the most succulent cuts of meat, the breasts of chicken or turkey are all used on a grand scale and in a country where the cost of living is high and wages low, this must seem all the more surprising. The fact, however, which emerges with most significance is the conservatism of the people. Certain dishes are regional and traditional: Aubergine Mousakka, Imam Bayildi, Baklava, Chicken Pilâv etc, and if the Turkish cook wants to make any of these dishes, whether for a family occasion or a special Bayram day, she will unhesitatingly use all the butter, cream, eggs and olive oil called for, never dreaming of substituting inferior ingredients. Imam Bayildi, for instance, requires just so much olive oil, etc, and if the recipe is altered even the merest fraction, it is *not* the dish which caused the original Imam to faint! I once asked my sister's cook in Istanbul why she used nine small eggs in the Revani she was making instead of six large ones. She replied without hesitation that the recipe called for nine *small* eggs. When questioned further she grew dumb with the inability to answer but allowed finally that when the recipe was first evolved (it was one of the many which came out of the Dolmabahçe Saray when the last Sultan was deposed) the nine small eggs were found to be more satisfactory than the six large ones! Further than that she would not go and she afterwards complained to my sister that I had become very 'Europeanised'. This fetish of tradition is a part of Turkey and Turkish cooking and some of the dishes are so old that nobody ever questions their make-up.

The craze for vitaminising food, for balancing meals so that the greatest dietetic value may be extracted, is lost on the Turks; for centuries they have served well balanced meals quite by accident. Experts on vegetable dishes for generations, it must be remembered that the Turks, an Oriental people, were familiar with the cultivation of vegetables long before Pizarro swept down on Peru and brought back knowledge of the potato, unknowingly vitaminised themselves by simply serving their vegetables in the liquor in which they were cooked.

Turks have always eaten better than any other people in the Eastern Mediterranean and quite early in Ottoman times they spread their cooking throughout the region as, later, the French were to spread their cooking

Turkish cooking

throughout Europe. This is not to say that French influence has not penetrated as far as Turkey; it has indeed, but mostly to Istanbul or Ankara and none of these dishes are sacred to the Turks, they have no great weight of tradition attached to them, no stories with which to regale guests, no nostalgic memories of the great days. An agricultural people, dour, emotional and with little sense of humour, conservative by nature rather than circumstances, the Turks have, since the 11th Century, been very much to the forefront in the affairs of the Middle East.

The 11th and 12th Centuries were, undoubtedly, periods of great activity during which the Sultans, the Royal master builders, the descendants of Alp Arslan, rivalled in the very heart of Asia Minor all the richness and artistry of the age of Pericles. The works of the great Seljuk Turks tell not only of local riches but of a time of prosperity during which the people had not only the leisure to produce their works of art but the encouragement as well. Food, naturally, took pride of place; where there is wealth the quality of food increases, and the great banquets of the early Turks produced many of the dishes we are still familiar with today. The whole roasted lamb or the young sucking calf stuffed with rice and exotic herbs, whilst never diminishing in appeal, gave way to more specialised dishes. The lamb and the calf were dissected and grilled chops (cooked over charcoal), kidneys ravished with butter and cream, kebabs wrapped in paper and cooked in pine kernels were discovered to have their appeal too. Rich in dress and ornamentation, succinct in speech, imbued with the knowledge of architecture, acquired undoubtedly in their migrations across Asia and half the face of the world, the early Turks liked their foods well spiced and highly seasoned. The spice trade originated with the Phoenicians; cane sugar was brought in by the Venetians in the 11th Century, the Turks, acquisitive, sampled everything.

Even today the Anatolian peasant lives somewhat better than his European counterpart. Turkey is still an agricultural country despite the reputation of her soldiers, and many of the regional dishes, Circassian Chicken, which comes to us from the mountainous Duzce, or Ankara Scoblianka, a product of the Tartars of old Ankara, come to us unchanged by time and are served in the hotels and restaurants (lokanta) of the big cities. Erzurum and Kars are regions rich in meat. Istanbul and the Black Sea coast give us fish unknown in any other part of the world. It might almost be said that life in Turkey revolves around food. Hours of long and patient effort are spent in the kitchens and in summer all meals are served in the open. Even in the shabbiest districts of old Istanbul each small house has its own veranda and its fig tree and perhaps an ancient vine or two and honeysuckle (most delicately named by the Turks 'hanim elk' – lady's hand) smothering the wire fences between the houses. Roughly hewn wooden tables are covered with fine linen cloths, relics of a great grandmother perhaps or made for the trousseau when the present middle aged cook was a newly betrothed girl of ten. Cloths, napkins, cushion covers are all heavily embroidered in exquisite patterns; rich Sparta carpets cover the floors even though there may scarcely be a stick of furniture to stand on them. It is a land of carpets and prayer rugs and no Turkish family would ever be put to the shame of being without one or the other. Table arrangements differ from the European. Knives are used only for meat, all other dishes are eaten with a fork or spoon. Meat and vegetables are quite distinct dishes, each with its own honour, and are served as separate courses.

In this book it will be seen that some vegetable dishes are served cold. In Turkey this always applies to any vegetable which has been cooked in olive oil. Meats, kebabs, chops, steaks, are regarded as being best when eaten alone and even pilâv, king of dishes, is handed separately. Very rarely except in some of the French inspired cooking, does pilav accompany the meat on the same plate.

Marketing is done daily and in the mornings, thus ensuring a continuously fresh supply of all perishable commodities. The markets are in the open and prices highly competitive, in a land of fruit, fruit is naturally very cheap. It is a hot country too and being Muslim in character, the people are most fastidious about cleanliness. All fruit is washed before being eaten, even a bare-footed street urchin, hungry as a wolf more than likely, will not eat the piece of melon or peach that he has picked up beside a fruit seller's stall until he has first washed it in the fountains of the local mosque. The fish markets are colourful, noisy with the cries of the vendors and gay with the rigging and the bright sails of the little fishing smacks. The fishermen wear gaily striped aprons and murderous knives attached to a broad leather belt in the middle. The markets stretch along the shores of the Golden Horn, where the mosques of the city reflect their sad nostalgic shadows and the sky in spring and summer is vivid cerulean. Here is a riot of colour and harmony, worth any visitor's attention if he doesn't mind getting his feet wet. The fish, freshly caught, lie in silver state, their scales a glistening iridescence, bright yellow lemons and emerald green parsley arranged symmetrically around them. Some of the fish look mysterious, blue and rose enamelled, too exotic to be subjected to dissection in the kitchen. The swordfish (kiliç) sherry brown, the mullet (barbunya) glitteringly orange silver, the turbot (kalkan) with its unexpected lime green bones and

Turkish cooking

exquisite white flesh, the mackerel (uskumru) line a pearl in its bed of vines leaves, tufts of curly endive decorating it with artistry, give intellectual nourishment as well as, later perhaps, physical.

Freshly killed meats come to the cities two and three times in a week and to soften them, the Turks pound them thin with a heavy mallet then steep them in onion juice for a day or two until the meat has tenderised.

Pastrycook shops dominate city, village and town. Apart from the local coffee shops, where old men sit mulling over the day's news, they are the most popular innovations of Turkish community life. It is almost agonising to choose where to buy one's baklava or lokma, each little shop seems to have a more mouth-watering display than the next. These shops are famous throughout the land, often being handed down from father to son for generations and the secrets of sweetmaking guarded jealously. Bayram days (religious festivals) have their own traditional sweets, of which baklava is the king. But Turkish Delight (lokum) and Kadingöbegi (lady's navel) are close seconds. Lokma is exclusively the going-to-school-for-the-first-time sweet. In the old days, it was hoped to induce a sweet temper in the Imam who was the teacher. Imams were reputed men of notoriously short tempers and incredible meanness, witness the delightful name of Imam Bayildi, literally, the Imam Fainted, so called because the original Imam, for whom the dish was created, is said to have fainted at the expense of the olive oil used in the making. Helva has less happy associations, being used on the fortieth day after a member of the family's death when, according to Muslim belief, the chin of the deceased drops. This, it is believed, causes great pain, so in order to lessen the pain special family prayers are said on that day and helva eaten in the name of the dead person. In the houses of the wealthy, great pots of helva are made and distributed amongst the poor. In this way it is hoped more prayers will be said and the dead will have nothing to complain about.

There is another popular sweet called Asure and here I shall be forgiven, I trust, if I quote briefly from my book *Portrait of a Turkish Family*. 'Asure is a sweet cooked with wheat, beans, figs, sultanas, dates, what you will, the whole being boiled for several hours until the result looks a little like aspic jelly. The legend of asure is that when Noah in the Ark found himself running short of supplies, he ordered all the remaining food to be cooked together for one last gigantic meal. This was asure, or so we are told. During the days of the Ottoman Empire a month used to be set aside each year for the making of asure in all the houses of the rich, who afterwards distributed it to the poor. When my grandfather was alive it used to be made in our house.' I remember it used to be made in a huge silver pot, copper lined, and for a whole day the house would be filled with the sweet, rather sickly smell of it. I have included it in this book rather as a relic of days that are gone and not in any expectation that anyone will make it – even in Turkey today the practice has dwindled, except amongst the very old who are still concerned with the welfare of their souls.

The sheep also figures symbolically in Turkish life. On the first morning of every Kurban Bayrami the rich slaughter a ewe or a ram (if the latter its horns are painted silver and gold and a red ribbon adorns its throat) to give to the poor of their district in the belief that on the Day of Judgement the rams (or ewes) slaughtered throughout their life to feed the poor will carry them across the Sirat Köprösü, a bridge between earth and heaven, sharper than a sword and thinner than a hair.

Birds are immune. There is no Turkish recipe for the tongues of larks, for ortolans, or for stuffed pigeon, in fact the latter are considered to be the little messengers of God and enjoy great freedom in the gardens of the mosques where they strut and preen and are grotesquely overfed.

There are many Turkish dishes, but I have tried to include here only the ones most likely to appeal to the European palate. Even so the task has been difficult, for Turkish cooking is very rich. Dolmas are heavy with stuffing, cooked either in oil or butter. Meats, braised or grilled or cooked with a vegetable, often come to table swimming in butter or sheep's fat. The famous Döner Kebab has been omitted (along with many other famous dishes) since most kitchens do not contain charcoal stoves or a revolving roasting spit.

The names of the dishes are almost always expressive, such as Kadin Budu, literally lady's thigh or Kadingöbegi, to be translated as lady's navel. The anatomy of the ladies has ever been a popular subject among the Turks.

It is with a certain pride, however, that I present this emasculated book of Turkish cooking, for many of the recipes are old family favourites, some of them were evolved by the 'fat Hacer' now, alas, dead and for whom I too ate helva hoping to lessen her pain in the new world. But all the recipes are old, even Hacer did no more than play upon a tradition, and the eating of a good plain pilâv differs in no appreciable way today from the days when, from across the fat rich pasturelands of Asia Minor, Sultan Mehmet in 1453 broke down the door of the Eastern Roman Empire.

It only remains for me to thank the many Turkish friends who yielded family secrets and also to add a special word of praise for my sister, Madame Muazzez Aretikin and my sister-in-law, Madame Bedia Orga, both of Istanbul, who have had the thankless task of testing a good many of these recipes.

Istanbul and London, 1955   9

Turkish cooking

Soups
Corbarlar

Almond Soup

Badem Corbasi

225g (8oz) ground sweet almonds
900ml (1½ pints) veal
(or lamb) stock
1 teaspoon coriander seed
1 teaspoon lemon rind

6 bitter almonds
450ml (¾ pint) single cream
6 large eggs
1 teaspoon salt

Hard-boil the eggs, remove the yolks and put in a mortar with the ground almonds and the bitter almonds, lemon rind and coriander seed. Pound thoroughly to a paste and mix with 225ml (8floz) of stock.

Put the rest of the stock in a heavy based saucepan and bring to the boil. Add the ground almond mixture, stir well and cook for 10 minutes on a low heat. Just before serving add the cream, reheat thoroughly but do not allow to come to the boil again.

Turkish cooking

Cream of Chicken Soup

Tavuk Corbasi

100–150g (4–5oz) cooked chicken
   breast
600ml (1 pint) chicken stock
50g (2oz) butter
140g (1½oz) sifted plain flour

Salt to taste
450ml (¾ pint) milk
225ml (8floz) single cream
6 asparagus heads
2 tablespoons chopped fresh chives

Snap off the tough stalks of the asparagus and remove the scales if sandy or
tough. Plunge upright, tied together loosely, into boiling salted water in a
deep saucepan and cook for 20–25 minutes. Remove from heat, drain and
keep hot.

Melt the butter in a pan, add the flour, salt, milk and stock and bring slowly
to the boil, stirring frequently. Boil for 2 minutes, then remove from the heat.

Put two thirds of the chicken breast in a mortar and pound into a paste.
Add to the stock mixture and force through a sieve. Return to the heat and
add the cream. Heat thoroughly but do not allow to boil again. Decorate
with the rest of the breast cut into fine strips, the asparagus heads and the
chopped chives. Serve at once.

Circassian Soup

Cerkes Corbasi

350g (12oz) sifted plain flour
1 egg
3 egg yolks
2 teaspoons salt
1.5 litres (2½ pints) chicken stock
450ml (¾ pint) single cream
700g (1½lb) cooked minced chicken
3 large onions

1 teaspoon white pepper
4 sprigs parsley
50g (2oz) butter
1 tablespoon finely chopped fresh
  mint
½ tablespoon chopped fresh thyme
½ teaspoon salt

Melt the butter and sauté the chopped onions until transparent. Add the chicken, parsley, salt and pepper and cook another 5 minutes. Remove from heat and cool.

Sift the flour and salt into a mixing bowl, make a well in the centre and add 1 egg yolk, the whole egg and a very little lemon water (equal proportions of lemon juice and iced water). Mix well and knead into a stiff dough. Cover the bowl with a damp cloth and leave the dough to 'rest' for 1 hour.

Roll out fairly thickly on a floured board. Now place the chicken mixture in teaspoons along the pastry, 2.5cm (1in) from the top edge and 1cm (½in) apart from each other. Fold the pastry over, seal with water and cut into squares. Repeat the operation until all the pastry and chicken mixture has been used.

Bring stock to boil, drop in the squares of pastry and simmer for 20–25 minutes with the lid on all the time.

Beat the remaining 2 egg yolks, combine with the cream and add to the soup at the end of the 25 minutes. Stir once, remove from heat immediately and serve with a garnishing of butter to which the thyme and mint have been added.

Turkish cooking

Meat Ball Soup

Köfte Corbasi

450g (1lb) finely minced lamb,
    uncooked
1 onion, minced
100g (4oz) long-grain rice
15g (½oz) melted butter
1 teaspoon each cayenne pepper
    and salt
A little water

1.2 litres (2 pints) beef or vegetable
    stock
225ml (8floz) wine (white for
    vegetable stock, red for beef stock)
2 egg yolks
Juice of 1 lemon
8 sprigs chopped fresh parsley

Put the stock into a pan with the wine, bring to the boil and reduce, uncovered, until 1.2 litres (2 pints) of the liquid are left. This will take some time, so reduce to the proper amount well beforehand.

Clean and wash the rice and boil for 15 minutes in plenty of boiling water salted water. Strain and allow to cool.

Into a mixing bowl put the lamb, onion, pepper, salt and cooked rice and mix well together with the hands. Shape into small balls, the size of a walnut, between wet palms and roll in the minced parsley. Arrange in layers in a heavy based saucepan and pour over them the wine and stock mixture and the butter. Boil gently for 30 minutes, then remove from heat. Mix the lemon juice with a very little water (about 1 tablespoon). Beat the egg yolks and combine gradually with the lemon juice. Pour this into the saucepan, away from the heat and off the boil, sprinkle over the remaining parsley and serve immediately in soup bowls.

Onion Soup

Sogan Corbasi

1.7 litres (3 pints) chicken stock
450g (1lb) finely chopped onions
40g (1½oz) butter
50g (2oz) sifted plain flour

225ml (8floz) single cream
50g (2oz) grated Gruyère cheese
2 tablespoons salt
Croutons of fried bread

Put the stock in a deep heavy based saucepan, add the onions and bring to boil. Simmer until the onions are soft, about 40 minutes. Strain through a sieve, forcing the onions through, and return the purée to the saucepan.

Melt the butter and add the flour, stirring all the time, and make a roux. Cook for 2–3 minutes. Thin down gradually with some of the stock, taking care that the mixture does not become lumpy. Add the cream gradually and pour into the purée, mixing thoroughly. Pour into individual cups, sprinkle with the Gruyère and brown very quickly under the grill. Serve the croutons of fried bread.

Turkish cooking

Palace Soup

Saray Corbasi

450g (1lb) button mushrooms
600 ml (1 pint) chicken stock
225ml (8floz) single cream
225ml (8floz) white wine
25g (1oz) plain flour
Croutons of fried bread

5 egg yolks
¼ teaspoon white pepper
1 teaspoon celery salt
40g (1½oz) butter
3 tablespoons chopped, fresh chives

Melt 1 tablespoon of the butter, add the flour and brown slightly. Add the stock by degrees, stirring all the time.

Slice the mushrooms in half and sauté in the rest of the butter. Add to stock and bring to boil slowly. Cook for about 40 minutes over a low heat. Remove from heat and add cream.

Beat the egg yolks, add wine and pour into the saucepan. Simmer for 1–2 minutes and serve at once with croutons of bread rolled in chopped fresh chives.

Red Lentil Soup

Kirmizî Mercimek Corbasi

1.7 litres (3 pints) vegetable stock
175g (6oz) red lentils
2 onions, chopped
1 teaspoon paprika
4 tablespoons chopped fresh parsley

15g (½oz) sifted plain flour
3 egg yolks
25g (1oz) butter
50ml (2floz) wine vinegar
225g (8floz) single cream

Melt 1 tablespoon of butter and fry the onions for 2 minutes. Add the cleaned lentils and 450ml (¾ pint) of water and boil until the lentils are tender (if more liquid is needed, use stock). Add the stock, salt and paprika, bring to the boil, then remove from the heat. Strain through a sieve, forcing lentils through, return to the pan and keep hot.

Make a roux with the rest of the butter and the flour and cook for about 2 minutes. Add the cream very gradually, away from the heat, stirring all the time. Add the well-beaten egg yolks and combine this mixture with the purée. Do not heat further but serve immediately, garnished with the croutons of bread rolled in the parsley.

Spoon over the wine vinegar at the table.

Turkish cooking

Tripe Soup

Iskembe Corbasi

900g (2lb) sheep's tripe
700g (1½ lb) cow's tripe
1.7 litres (3 pints) water
Rind and juice of 1 lemon
3 cloves garlic
125ml (4floz) beef stock
40g (1½oz) butter
Salt to taste

2 egg yolks
50ml (2floz) dry white wine
3 teaspoons paprika
1 teaspoon sweet marjoram
⅛ teaspoon thyme
125ml (4floz) single cream
25g (1oz) sifted plain flour

Scrape, clean and wash the tripe very thoroughly and cut into large pieces. Put into a heavy based saucepan with the lemon rind, herbs, garlic and salt. Cover with hot water, bring to boil then simmer for about 6 hours, skimming from time to time, and adding more *hot* water if necessary. Remove the tripe, cool slightly then cut into 2.5cm (1in) pieces. Strain the liquid in which it was cooked, then add the cubes of tripe and reheat very slowly. Melt a third of the butter, add the flour and cook for 1 minute, stirring all the time. Remove from the heat and thin with a little of the stock. Stir in the well-beaten egg yolks and add the lemon juice, a few drops at a time, stirring continuously. Add to the saucepan, mix well, raise the heat a little and bring to the boil. Remove at once from the heat, add the wine and a few pieces of mashed garlic, if liked.

Melt the rest of the butter and when just sizzling add the paprika. Remove from the heat and combine well.

Serve the soup in earthenware bowls with the butter/paprika mixture spooned over them.

Wedding Soup

Düğün Corbasi

450g (1lb) lamb	75g (3oz) plain flour
2.8 litres (5 pints) water	1 large carrot
75g (3oz) butter	1 large onion, chopped
1 lemon	3 egg yolks
1 teaspoon salt	2 teaspoons paprika
125ml (4floz) white wine	1 teaspoon cinnamon

Trim the meat and marinate in the wine for 6 hours. Drain off and put into a large heavy based saucepan with the carrot and the chopped onion. Add the water and the wine in which meat was marinated. Simmer very gently for 4 hours, removing any scum as it rises to the top. Remove the meat and strain the stock into another saucepan. Cut the meat into strips, julienne fashion, and add to the stock.

Melt half the butter in another pan, add the sifted flour and cook gently for 3–4 minutes, stirring continuously. Do not allow the flour to brown. Remove from the heat and thin gradually with a little of the stock, taking great care at this stage that no lumps form. When it is thinned sufficiently, pour into the meat stock and stir well. Bring slowly to the boil.

Whisk the egg yolks with the salt, add the juice of the lemon gradually and 225–450ml (8floz–¾ pint) of stock. Stir well. Remove stock from the heat, allow to go off the boil then add the egg mixture, combining well.

Melt the rest of the butter and mix in the paprika.

When serving the soup, spoon the butter and paprika mixture over each bowl and dust with cinnamon.

Turkish cooking

Fish
Baliklar

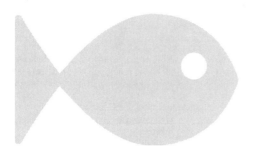

Baked Bass

Levrekbalagi Gratan

900g (2lb) whole bass	450ml (3/4 pint) white wine
1 bay leaf	1 sprig parsley
40g (1½oz) butter	15g (½oz) plain
100g (4oz) grated Cheddar cheese	1½ teaspoons paprika
Salt and pepper to taste	

Clean the inside of the fish and wash well. Put in a greased baking tin, pour the wine over and add the crushed bay leaf and parsley sprig. Cook in a hot oven 230°C/450°F/Gas 8 for 50 minutes, turning after 25 minutes and basting frequently with the wine. Remove from the oven, take out the fish and leave to keep warm.

Melt a third of the butter, add the flour and cook until slightly browned, about 3–4 minutes. Add the rest of the butter and stir until smooth. Remove the bay leaf and parsley sprig from the liquor, strain, and add this to the flour and butter, stirring all the time. Cook until thick. Add the paprika and the cheese, stir well and cook for another 2 minutes. Remove from the heat and spread this mixture over the fish. Brown under the grill and serve immediately.

Turkish cooking

Carp in Wine

Sarapli Sazanbaligi

2 medium sized carp
125ml (4floz) tarragon vinegar
175g (6oz) sultanas
125ml (4floz) red wine
Salt and pepper
Chopped fresh parsley

1 onion, chopped
6–7 peppercorns
100g (4oz) finely chopped walnuts
15ml (½floz) lemon juice
Enough fish stock to cover fish

Clean and cut the fish into pieces. Salt each piece, smother with onion juice and leave in a cool place for 1 hour.

Cook the pieces of fish in the fish stock on a low heat until tender, this will not take very long as carp is a soft fish. Remove the fish and keep warm.

Add to the stock the sultanas, walnuts, wine and lemon juice and heat through, then boil rapidly and reduce liquor by half. Pour over the fish and serve garnished with thin lemon slices and chopped fresh parsley.

Red Gurnard

Mercanbaligi

900g (2lb) red gurnet	75g (3oz) butter
125ml (4floz) dry white wine	75g (3oz) button mushrooms
24 cooked shrimps	1 onion
1 tablespoon chopped fresh sorrel	½ bay leaf
600ml (1 pint) water	25g (1oz) plain flour
225ml (8floz) single cream	125ml (4floz) water
100g (4oz) grated Cheddar cheese	1 diced carrot
Salt and pepper to taste	

Clean and fillet the fish and cut into 6 pieces. Wash well and arrange at the bottom of a greased saucepan.

Put the heads, bones and tails into a separate saucepan and all the vegetables, except the mushrooms. Add 600ml (1 pint) of the water and simmer for 2½ hours. Strain and keep the liquor in a warm place.

Clean the mushrooms and add to the fish in the saucepan, add wine and fish stock and cook for 20–25 minutes on a moderate heat. Remove the fish and the mushrooms and reduce the liquor by half by rapid, uncovered boiling. Strain and keep hot.

Melt 15g (½oz) of the butter and fry the flour in it for 3 minutes. Add the cream gradually, stirring all the time, then add the reduced stock by degrees. Cook until nicely thickened, stirring all the time. Add the rest of the butter and stir again. Add cheese and seasoning and cook for 2 minutes, still stirring. Remove from heat.

Skin the fish and separate into small pieces, add shrimps, mushrooms and half the cheese sauce and mix well. Arrange in a serving dish in the shape of a fish and spread the rest of the sauce over it. Sprinkle with a little more cheese and brown under a grill. Serve hot.

Turkish cooking

Mackerel in Olive Oil

Uskumru Pilâkisi

4 medium-sized mackerel
5 cloves of garlic, halved
5 onions, thinly sliced
1 tablespoon tomato ketchup
125ml (4floz) dry white wine

175ml (6floz) olive oil
1 teaspoon paprika
1 thinly sliced carrot
450ml (¾ pint) fish stock
Salt to taste

Scale and clean the insides of the fish. Do not remove the heads or tails. Heat half the oil in a wide-bottomed pan, add the onions and cook for 15 minutes over a medium heat. Add the carrot and garlic and cook for a further 15 minutes. Remove the pan from the heat and add the rest of the oil, paprika, tomato ketchup, wine and seasoning. Cover and cook for another 20 minutes on a moderate heat. Uncover and boil fiercely for 7 minutes to reduce liquor, and remove from the heat again. Strain through muslin.

Arrange the mackerel side by side in the liquor, cover with a napkin and then put on the lid. Cook on a medium heat for 20–25 minutes then remove from the heat and allow to cool in the pan.

Serve very cold.

Stuffed Mackerel

Uskumru Dolmasi

4 large mackerel
3 eggs
6 sprigs dill
2 sprigs fresh mint
50g (2oz) fresh or bottled
   blackcurrants
75g (3oz) breadcrumbs
½ teaspoon coriander seed

450ml (¾ pint) olive oil
450g (1lb) onions
6 sprigs parsley
100g (4oz) pine kernels
100g (4oz) plain flour
2 teaspoons mixed herbs
Salt and pepper

Clean out the insides of the fish and wash well. Starting from the tail, rub the fish upwards with two fingers, exerting slight pressure all the time but taking care not to break the skin. Continue like this until the flesh inside has worked itself loose from the skin. Make a very small incision in the throat of the fish and through here work out the loose flesh and the backbone. It is during this part of the operation that care should be taken not to break the tender skin of the fish. Remember that to disembody the fish, pressure should be exerted *gently* from the tail upwards.

When the fish skins are completely emptied throw away the bones and chop the flesh into small pieces and put aside.

Put half the olive oil in a pan and fry the chopped onions until slightly browned. Add the pieces of fish, pine kernels, blackcurrants, mixed herbs, coriander and seasoning and cook for 6–7 minutes. Add the chopped dill, parsley and mint, mix well and remove from the heat. Allow to cool slightly then stuff the skins of the fish with this mixture, tightly and firmly but not too bulging or the skin will break. Then pull down the head of the fish slightly so that the incision in the throat is partly covered and the stuffing will not escape in the cooking.

Roll the stuffed fish in flour, then in beaten egg and lastly in the breadcrumbs. Fry them in the rest of the olive oil on a low heat until both sides are a rich golden brown.

Serve when completely cold.

Turkish cooking

Grey Mullet

Kefalbaligi Kâgitta

6 small grey mullet
75g (3oz) button mushrooms,
    halved
1 carrot, diced
125ml (4floz) fish stock

Greaseproof paper
50ml (2floz) olive oil
White part of 1 leek, chopped
225ml (8floz) dry white wine
Salt and pepper to taste

Grease a baking tin with butter.

Clean out the fish well, wash, and from the head downwards slit the back and remove the backbone carefully. Wash again, pat dry and lay side by side in the baking tin.

Heat the oil and fry the mushrooms, carrot and leek for 4–5 minutes. Add the wine, stock, salt and pepper and cook for about 20 minutes or until the vegetables are tender. Remove the vegetables and put on the fish, cover with double greaseproof paper and cook at 190°C/375°F/Gas 5 for 20 minutes.

Reduce the liquor by two thirds by rapid, uncovered boiling, strain and just before serving pour this over the fish.

Red Mullet

Kagitta Barbunya

6 medium-sized red mullet
50ml (2floz) olive oil
4 sprigs chopped fresh parsley
Greaseproof paper

75g (3oz) butter
Juice of 1 lemon
Verbena salt

Clean, wash and pat the fish dry, leaving on the heads and tails. Make a small slit in one side and clean out the insides thoroughly, wash well under running water.

Take double greaseproof paper and brush well with melted butter. Wrap the fish in this, secure with string, place on a baking sheet and cook at 230°C/450°F/Gas 8 for 40–50 minutes.

Mix the parsley, lemon juice, olive oil and salt and sprinkle over the fish just before serving.

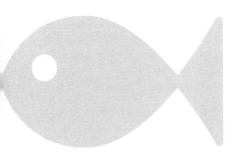

Turkish cooking

Stuffed Mussels

Midye Dolmasi

24 large mussels
225ml (8floz) olive oil
1 large tomato, skinned
15g (½oz) blackcurrants
1 teaspoon white pepper
½ teaspoon coriander seed
½ teaspoon chopped fresh thyme
Salt to taste

225g (8oz) long-grain rice
450g (1lb) onions, chopped
15g (½oz) pine kernels
½ teaspoon sugar
1 teaspoon chopped fresh chervil
½ teaspoon poppy seed
½ teaspoon chopped fresh basil

Wash the rice, cover with very hot water and leave aside until the water is quite cold. Wash several times under cold running water. Scrape and clean the mussels thoroughly then with a sharp knife open them. Clean off the hairs inside and after washing them leave aside in a tray of coarse salt.

Heat the oil and fry the onions for 6–7 minutes. Add the rice, pine kernels and salt, cover pan and fry for 20 minutes, stirring frequently. Add 125ml (4floz) of tomatoes, blackcurrants, herbs and pepper, mix well, cover pan and cook for another 10–12 minutes. Add the sugar, mix and remove from heat. Stuff the mussels with this mixture and arrange in layers in a wide-based pan. Add 225ml (8floz) of water, cover pan tightly and cook over a medium heat for 30–35 minutes. Remove the pan from the heat and allow the mussels to cool in their own liquor.

Serve very cold but just before serving dry the outsides of the mussels in a napkin and brush them over with olive oil to make them shine.

Shrimp Soufflé

Teke Suflesi

100g (4oz) butter
6 egg whites
90ml (3floz) milk
½ teaspoon salt

6 egg yolks
25g (3oz) plain flour
90ml (3floz) double cream
36 cooked shrimps

Melt the butter on a low heat, add the yolk of 1 egg and beat until smooth. Add, one by one, beating well after each ingredient, one sixth of the flour and milk. Repeat the process until all the yolks, flour and milk have been used. Stir well once and add the cream and salt.

Beat the egg whites until holding a peak and fold in carefully.

Grease a soufflé dish, line with the shrimps and a little more than half fill with the egg mixture. Bake at 190°C/375°F/Gas 5 until set and pale gold in colour. Serve at once, taking care the soufflé does not fall.

Turkish cooking

Meat and Poultry
Et ve Tavuklar

Ankara Scoblianka

Ankaranin Scobliankasi

700g (1½lb) veal steak
1 large onion, grated
225ml (8floz) single cream
Dash of paprika

75g (3oz) butter
6 mushrooms, sliced
Salt
1 tablespoon red or white wine

Cut the veal into thin strips, julienne fashion, flour lightly and sauté in half the butter until tender, shaking the pan frequently to prevent burning, and taking care the strips do not break.

Sauté the onion in the remaining butter until transparent but not brown, add the mushrooms and cook for another 7–8 minutes on moderate heat until the onions are pale brown and the mushrooms are well cooked. Remove from the heat and leave aside.

Remove the cooked veal from the pan, add 15g (½oz) of plain flour to the butter left in it and stir until smooth. Add the wine and salt and allow to bubble, stirring all the time to prevent lumps forming. Add the cream gradually and reduce the heat, stir until the sauce thickens then add the onions and the mushrooms. Add the veal last of all. Serve hot, sprinkled with paprika.

Turkish cooking

Beef Balls

Köfte

450g (1lb) minced beef, or lamb
1 egg
75g (3oz) breadcrumbs
1 teaspoon garlic salt
½ teaspoon chopped fresh dill
Vegetable oil for frying

2 egg yolks
Juice of 1 large onion
1 teaspoon white pepper
25g (1oz) plain flour
½ teaspoon chopped fresh sorrel

Prepare flour, breadcrumbs and the well-beaten egg, in separate dishes. Mix and knead for 10 minutes all the other ingredients, including the egg yolks. Form into flattened balls, dip in flour, then egg mixture, then breadcrumbs and fry in sizzling oil on a very low heat until well browned, about 10–12 minutes.

Serve hot with plain pilâv.

Beef with Macaroni

Dana etli Makarna

900g (2lb) sirloin of beef, or
   lamb fillet
225ml (8floz) red wine
5 peppercorns
2 bay leaves
2 chopped onions
Salt and pepper

50ml (2floz) vegetable oil
225ml (8floz) vegetable stock
2 cloves of garlic
1 diced carrot
3 tomatoes, skinned and seeded
225g (8oz) macaroni

Melt the oil in a deep heavy based saucepan and fry the meat for 10–15 minutes on a very high heat. Reduce the heat, add carrot, onions, garlic, bay leaves and peppercorns and cook for a further 10 minutes. Add tomatoes and cook for another 5 minutes. Add the wine and after 2 minutes add the stock.

Cook in the oven for 2 hours at 150°C/300°F/Gas 2, turning the meat at the end of the first hour. Remove the meat, slice, arrange on a serving dish and keep hot. Strain the liquid and keep hot, having first reduced by half.

Throw the macaroni into boiling salted water and cook for 20–25 minutes. Strain, wash quickly under running water and arrange round the meat on the dish. Pour the reduced liquid over the macaroni and serve at once.

Turkish cooking

Chicken in Aspic

Jelatinli Tavuk

275g (10oz) cooked diced chicken
1 teaspoon salt
50g (2oz) stuffed green olives
2 tablespoons gelatin
450ml (¾ pint) boiling water to`
   which has been added the
   rind of 1 lemon

125ml (4floz) mayonnaise
25g (1oz) toasted slivered almonds
50g (2oz) black grapes
30ml (1floz) white wine
225ml (8floz) mayonnaise, for
   serving
90ml (8floz) whipped cream

Strain the water and lemon rind through muslin and dissolve the gelatin. Add the wine and leave side to cool.

When partially set add the chicken, 125ml (4floz) of mayonnaise, salt, almonds, olives and grapes. When partially set again pour into a tube mould (wetted) and chill until firm. Unmould on a serving dish and surround with crisped cos lettuce (use ice water for crisping) and endives. Fill centre of tube with cottage cheese balls (mix 1½ teaspoons chervil with 225g (8oz) of cream cheese for this).

Serve with the extra mayonnaise mixed with the whipped cream.

To make mayonnaise for this dish:

125ml (4floz) olive oil
¼ teaspoon salt
⅛ teaspoon dry mustard
40g (1½oz) plain flour

50ml (2floz) water
50ml (2floz) tarragon vinegar
⅛ teaspoon sugar
1 egg

Put the dry ingredients in a saucepan, add vinegar and water, stir well, and cook over a low heat until the mixture starts to bubble. Boil for 2–3 minutes, stirring continuously. Remove from heat, cool thoroughly, add the egg and beat well for about 1 minute. Add the oil gradually, beating continuously until all the oil is absorbed. Chill before serving.

Chicken à la Bursa

Bursa Tavugu

900g–1.4kg (2–3lb) young chicken
3 large onions
Bunch of mixed herbs tied in
   muslin bag
30ml (1floz) single cream
1 tablespoon capers

90ml (3floz) olive oil
450ml (¾ pint) chicken stock
15g (½oz) plain flour
100g (4oz) stuffed green olives
1 tablespoon chopped fresh
   parsley

Cut the chicken into serving pieces and slice the onions. Heat the oil to boiling point, reduce heat and add the pieces of chicken and the onions and fry until a pale golden brown. Add the stock and the herbs and cook very gently until the chicken is tender. Remove the herbs and chicken.

Mix the flour with the cream, pour into the stock and cook for a few minutes, stirring all the time. Add garlic salt. Add the olives and the capers and cook for another 3 minutes.

Pour over the chicken and serve at once, garnished with parsley with a plain pilâv accompaniment.

Turkish cooking

Circassian Chicken

Cerkes Tavugu

450g–1.4kg (1–3lb) chicken
225ml (8floz) chicken stock
2 large onions, quartered
2 stalks celery
50g (2oz) breadcrumbs
½ teaspoon chopped fresh chervil
1 egg

1.7 litres (3 pints) water
225g (8oz) shelled walnuts
1 carrot, sliced
1 teaspoon sage
½ tablespoon paprika
½ teaspoon chopped fresh basil
Salt and pepper

Clean the chicken and put in a large saucepan with the onions, carrot, celery, herbs and salt. Bring to the boil slowly, skimming frequently. Reduce the heat and simmer for about 2¼–2½ hours until tender. Remove the chicken, strain liquor and put aside.

Remove all the meat from the chicken and shred into very small pieces.

Pound the walnuts in a mortar, add 1 tiny onion (finely minced), paprika and breadcrumbs and mix well together, pounding thoroughly. Add the chicken stock very gradually and mix to a stiffish paste. Add the egg, unbeaten, and leave aside for 15 minutes. Add the shredded chicken and stir well.

Shape the mixture into cutlets, dip in beaten egg and breadcrumbs and fry in a little hot butter until delicately browned on both sides. Serve hot with almond pilâv.

Chicken Curry

Hind Tavugu

1 large onion, chopped
1 teaspoon green ginger
40g (1½oz) butter
90ml (3floz) single cream
450g–1.4kg (1–3lb) minced
    boiled chicken
3 hard-boiled eggs
4 tablespoons chopped fresh mint
2 tablespoons chopped fresh parsley

1 teaspoon mashed garlic
2 tablespoons curry powder
450ml (¾ pint) chicken stock
4 tablespoons mayonnaise
225g (8oz) cooked long-grain rice
3 large tomatoes, skinned
2 tablespoons chopped fresh dill
1 sprig basil
1 tablespoon preserved ginger

Melt the butter and fry the onion, garlic and green ginger until pale golden brown in colour. Add the curry powder, season and cook on a low heat for 3–4 minutes. Add the chicken stock, boil and stir until it begins to thicken slightly. Add the chicken and cook slowly until dry but not too dry, the mixture should be barely moist but not at the sticking stage.

Allow to cool, mixing in the preserved ginger when half cool.

Mix in the cream and the mayonnaise and put in a ring mould and chill until set. Serve well-chilled with plain boiled rice and garnish with the sliced eggs, sliced tomatoes and the fresh herbs, finely chopped. Fill the centre of the mould with pitted black olives and a little more preserved ginger, all sprinkled with lemon juice.

Chicken Macaroni

Makarna Tavuklu

225g (8oz) macaroni
75g (3oz) butter
4 slices of tongue
225ml (8floz) single cream
1 teaspoon white pepper
25g (3oz) cooked green peas
Salt to taste
40g (1½oz) buttered crumbs

Boiling water
100–150g (4–5oz) breast of boiled
 chicken
25g (1oz) plain flour
Sprig of rosemary
1 tablespoon grated fresh coconut
75g (3oz) chopped mushrooms,
 boiled for 5 minutes

Cook the macaroni in the boiling water for 20 minutes, strain, wash under hot water and leave aside to keep warm.

Melt half the butter, add the flour and cook for 3 minutes without browning, stirring all the time. Add the cream slowly and boil for 2 more minutes, taking care the cream does not stick. Add the coconut and seasoning, stir well and remove from heat.

Cut the chicken breast and tongue into strips, julienne fashion, and add to the cream mixture. Add the peas and rosemary, stir and leave beside the heat.

Grease a baking tray and arrange half the cooked macaroni in it, pour the sauce over and add the rest of the macaroni. Garnish with the mushrooms. Spread the buttered crumbs over the top, dot generously with butter and cook until golden brown in a very hot oven (230°C/450°F/Gas 8). Serve hot.

Grilled Chops

Pirzola

900g (2lb) lamb chops
1 tablespoon olive oil
Garlic salt

1 tablespoon white wine
1 tablespoon chopped fresh thyme
Juice only of 1 onion

Clean and trim all the fat off the chops, then pound the meat until it is less than half its original thickness.

Arrange on a large plate and pour over them the wine, onion juice and oil. Sprinkle with the thyme and the garlic salt and leave aside for 2 hours in a cool place, turning them at the end of 1 hour. Drain but do not wipe. Grill until nicely browned on both sides (about 8 minutes). Serve with pilâv.

Turkish cooking

Steamed Chops

Patatesli bugu Pirzolasi

900g (2lb) lamb chops
50ml (2floz) vegetable oil
2 tomatoes, skinned and sliced
225g (8oz) potatoes
Garlic salt to taste

50g (2oz) plain flour
175ml (6floz) thin vegetable stock
1 large onion
1 teaspoon black pepper
2 tablespoons chopped fresh dill

Clean and trim the chops and pound with an iron mallet until less than half their original thickness. Arrange in a layer in a wide-based saucepan.

Cut the onion into very thin slices and place on top of the chops, add the tomatoes, the potatoes cut into thin rounds and the dill. Season with the salt and pepper and add the stock. Cover the pan tightly. Make a thick pastry with the flour and a little water and seal the edges of the lid thoroughly. Cook over a gentle heat for 20 minutes, then increase heat a little and cook for a further 2½ hours.

Remove the pastry from the lid and serve hot after 7–8 minutes' 'rest'.

Countryman's Kebab

Bahcevan Kebabi

900g (2lb) leg of lamb
75g (3oz) butter
40 button onions
2 sliced carrots
2 large tomatoes, skinned

175g (6oz) fresh green peas
2 pimentos, cut up
3 tablespoons chopped fresh dill
600ml (1 pint) chicken stock
Garlic salt

Cut the meat into small pieces. Melt the butter and cook the meat over slow heat for 15 minutes. Add the carrots, cover and cook for 1 hour, still on a low heat, shaking the pan occasionally to prevent burning. Add the cut up tomatoes, onions, pimentos, green peas and salt. Add a third of the stock every 30 minutes and cook for 1¾ hours. Add the dill at the last minute, stir once and then serve with plain pilâv.

Note: This dish is especially delicious if served in the traditional Turkish peasant-style, that is, adding a few spoonfuls yogurt at the table and sprinkling lightly with paprika.

Turkish cooking

Lamb Kebab en Papilotte

Kâgit Kebab

900g (2lb) leg of lamb
2 chopped onions
1 large tomato, skinned
2 tablespoons chopped fresh dill
2 carrots, diced
225g (8oz) margarine
1 teaspoon white pepper

75g (3oz) cooked green peas
30ml (1floz) vegetable oil
50ml (2floz) dry white wine
2 tablespoons chopped fresh thyme
2 potatoes
1 teaspoon salt
Greaseproof paper

Cut the meat into fairly large pieces and fry in the margarine until the both sides are pink. Remove from the heat and leave aside. Add onions, carrots, half of the dill, salt and pepper and cook over a gentle heat for 25 minutes. Add the wine and tomatoes and cover with greaseproof paper. Cover and cook for 1 hour more. Take out the meat and the carrots and keep hot, separately.

Cut the potatoes into thin round slices and sauté in the oil for 5–6 minutes. Add them to the carrots, green peas and thyme.

Take some fresh greaseproof paper (cut more than twice the size of each piece of meat) and put a piece of meat in the centre. Cover with enough of the vegetables, pour over a little sauce and bring the ends of the paper together so that everything is well sealed and the sauce cannot escape and twist the ends securely.

Lay the envelopes of greaseproof paper on a baking tray side by side, sprinkle with a little water and bake for 20 minutes at 230°C/450°F/Gas 8. Serve hot with spring pilâv.

Kebab in Puff Pastry

Talas Kebab

450g (1lb) puff pastry
225ml (8floz) chicken stock
25g (1oz) butter
1 teaspoon white pepper
½ teaspoon chopped fresh tarragon
1 large egg

450g (1lb) boned chicken
3 onions, thinly sliced
1 tablespoon tomato purée
1 teaspoon chopped fresh chervil
2 tablespoons chopped fresh parsley
Salt to taste

To make the pastry (old Turkish recipe):

450g (1lb) plain flour, sifted 5 times
Just under 225ml (8floz) cold
    water to which 1 tablespoon of
    dry white wine has been added

450g (1lb) butter

Remember that all utensils, ingredients and hands should be quite cold. First sieve the flour (this will be the sixth time) into a mixing bowl. Cut the butter into 60–70 small cubes. Separate the cubes and with the tips of the fingers mix lightly into the flour. With a large spoon mix in the water/wine mixture and stir together until the mixture leaves the sides of the bowl. Turn out onto a well-floured marble slab and rolling away from you all the time with small, quick forward movements, shape into an oblong. This is the most important part of the whole operation so make quite certain that every part of the pastry is rolled evenly. Take hold of the top two corners and fold down to within a third of the bottom edge. Now fold the bottom corners up to the top so that you have a neat slab of pastry, three layers in thickness. Turn the pastry to the right, this gives you a folded edge on the left and right sides and leaves the two open edges facing you and away from you. Roll out and fold again as before. Do this 6 times in all then put into the fridge immediately. Do not use before 5 hours and, if possible, leave overnight.

Turkish cooking

To make filling:

Melt the butter in a heavy based saucepan and cut the chicken into long thin pieces and cook in the butter for 5 minutes. Add the onions, stir once, cover and cook for 15 minutes, shaking the pan occasionally to prevent sticking. Uncover and cook for a further 10 minutes. Add the stock, tomato purée and salt, cover and cook on a very low heat for 2 hours. Add pepper and all the herbs, stir well, remove from the heat and cool.

Cut the puff pastry into small pieces and roll out to 15cm (6in) squares. Place some of the chicken mixture in the centre of each square, fold the pastry crosswise into a triangular shape, seal with a little beaten egg and put on a lightly greased baking tray. Glaze with beaten egg and bake at 190°C/325°F/Gas 5 for 30 minutes.

Rabbit Kebab

Tavsan Kebabi

1 plump rabbit
450ml (¾ pint) red wine
225ml (8floz) olive oil
1 teaspoon white pepper
2 bay leaves, crumbled
5 cloves
6 cloves garlic

Juice of 1 large lemon
1 teaspoon salt
1 teaspoon chopped fresh mint
3 tablespoons finely choped fresh
  parsley
65g (2½oz) butter

Wash and clean the rabbit and leave the liver on one side. Stud the rabbit with ccloves and a few pieces of garlic.

Mix together two thirds of the wine, olive oil, mint, bay leaves and parsley and marinate the rabbit in this for 24 hours, turning occasionally. Remove the rabbit, drain but do not dry and grill on a very large skewer for 1½ hours, turning continuously to avoid burning.

Melt the butter, chop the liver finely and add to the melted butter with the remaining garlic which must also have been chopped. Sauté for 2–3 minutes, shaking the pan to prevent sticking. Remove from the heat, cool slightly and pound into a paste in a mortar. Add the rest of the wine gradually, the lemon juice, salt and pepper. Transfer to a heavy based saucepan and over a low heat bring to simmering point, stirring all the time with a wooden spoon.

Pour this sauce over the grilled rabbit and serve immediately, with plain pilâv.

Turkish cooking

Shashlik

Saslik

900g (2lb) leg of lamb
225g (8floz) olive oil
275g (10oz) button mushrooms
Skewers

4 finely chopped onions
6 large spring onions
Salt and paprika

Cut the meat from the bone, remove the skin and fat and cut into cubes. (Incidentally, the bones, skin and fat in this dish and in all the shish kebab dishes can be used as a basis for stocks.)

Marinate the meat cubes in olive oil, salt and paprika for 24–36 hours (the longer the better). Allow 6 pieces of meat to each skewer, 1cm (½in) apart, and grill for 5–6 minutes, turning all the time.

Sauté the mushrooms in the olive oil which was used for marinating and serve as a garnish with the pieces of lamb. Cut the spring onions up very small and scatter over the whole dish.

Shish Kebab I

Sis Kebabi

900g (2lb) leg of mutton
Juice of 1 large onion
Shish kebab skewers

1 tablespoon olive oil
Salt to taste

Cut the meat from the bones, remove the skin and fat and cut into cubes. Put them in a bowl with the onion juice and the olive oil and leave for 3 hours. Allow 6 pieces of meat to each skewer, place them 1cm (½in) apart from each other and grill for 5–6 minutes, turning all the time. Remove from the skewer at table and serve with pilâv.

Note: Sliced green peppers, tomatoes and onion rings may be served as a garnish but these *must* be grilled on separate skewers. If they are included on the meat skewer the meat becomes tough and this is the reason why so many shish kebab dishes served in restaurants outside the Middle East are tough and unpalatable.

Turkish cooking

Shish Kebab II

Sis Kebabi

900g (2lb) leg of lamb
2 cloves of garlic pounded in a
    mortar

Salt
225ml (8floz) dry white wine
25g (1oz) butter

Cut the meat from the bones, remove the skin and fat and cut the meat into cubes. Marinate in the wine and the pounded garlic for 6–8 hours. Allow 6 pieces of lamb for each skewer, 1cm (½in) apart from each other. Brush well with melted butter and grill for 5–6 minutes, turning continuously. Serve hot with stuffed tomatoes.

String Kebab

Kaytan Kebabi

450g (1lb) leg of mutton (without
   fat or bones)
50ml (2floz) dry white wine
¼ teaspoon salt
¼ teaspoon nutmeg
¼ teaspoon chopped fresh rosemary
25g (1oz) butter
½ tablespoon chopped fresh dill

1 large onion, grated
¼ teaspoon white pepper
¼ teaspoon cinnamon
¼ teaspoon ground cloves
1 tablespoon grated coconut
2 tablespoons chopped fresh parsley
1 bunch spring onions

Cut the meat into pieces, 7.5cm (3in) long by 1cm (½in) wide. Put in a bowl
and add the onions, salt, pepper and wine. Mix well and leave aside for 12
hours. Put each piece of meat on a skewer and grilled one side for 3 minutes
and the other side for 2 minutes.

Mix together the melted butter, coconut, herbs and spices and whilst the
meat is being grilled keep brushing with this mixture.

Serve hot sprinkled with parsley, dill and spring onions with a plain pilâv
accompaniment.

Tas Kebab

900g (2lb) leg of mutton (top part)
2 chopped onions
1 teaspoon white pepper
450ml (¾ pint) lamb stock

40g (1½oz) butter
2 tomatoes, chopped and skinned
1 level teaspoon chopped fresh
  thyme
Salt to taste

Cut the meat, freed of fat, into small cubes, sprinkle with pepper and the thyme and leave aside for 4 hours.

Melt the butter and fry the onions for 5 minutes. Add the meat, cover the pan tightly, reduce the heat to *very low* and cook for 20 minutes, shaking the pan occasionally to prevent sticking but not uncovering.

Add the tomatoes to the meat and onions, with salt to taste and half the stock. Cook on a low heat for 2½ hours until the meat is very tender, adding the remaining stock at the end of the first hour of cooking.

For the last 15 minutes of cooking time, uncover, increase the heat and boil rapidly until the liquid is reduced to a few tablespoons.

Serve with pilâv.

Veal Tas Kebab

Dana Etli Tas Kebabi

900g (2lb) leg of veal (top part)
225ml (8floz) dry white wine
2 tomatoes, skinned and chopped
1 bay leaf
¼ teaspoon ground cinnamon
2 tablespoon fresh coconut,
   shredded

30ml (1floz) vegetable oil
2 minced onions
1 teaspoon pepper
¼ teaspoon ground cloves
¼ teaspoon chopped fresh thyme
1 teaspoon salt

Cut the meat into pieces the size of a walnut. Put into a heavy based saucepan with the onions, salt, coconut, bay leaf, thyme, cinnamon, pepper and cloves. Mix well and leave for 2 hours in a cool place.

Add the oil to the meat cubes in the saucepan. Sauté for 3–4 minutes, shaking the pan continuously. Add the tomatoes and the wine. Cover tightly and cook over a low heat for 4 hours.

Serve immediately with saffron pilâv.

Turkish cooking

Chicken Kofte

Tavuk Köftesi

450g (1lb) cooked chicken breast
4 egg yolks
50g (2oz) plain flour
½ teaspoon sweet marjoram
3 slices tongue
225g (8oz) butter

225ml (8floz) single cream
40g (1½oz) butter
½ teaspoon white pepper
6 chopped mushrooms
25g (1oz) grated Gruyère cheese
Salt to taste

Cook the mushrooms in boiling salted water for 10 minutes. Remove from the heat, drain and allow to cool.

Mince the chicken breast very finely. Melt the butter, add the flour and cook without browning for 3 minutes. Add the cream gradually, stirring all the time, the well-beaten egg yolks, cheese and salt. Cook, stirring continuously, until the mixture is very stiff. Add the chicken, mushroom and the tongue, cut into very small pieces. Mix well, remove from the heat and leave aside to cool.

Take small pieces of this mixture, about the size of a walnut, shape into flattish balls and fry in hot butter until golden brown on both sides, starting with a very low heat and gradually increasing.

Serve hot with plain pilâv.

Fried Kofte

Tavada Köfte

450g (1lb) beef, or lamb	1 teaspoon cayenne pepper
3 slices stale bread	2 eggs
2 grated onions	1 tablespoon chopped fresh dill
2 cloves garlic	40g (1½oz) Gruyère cheese
50ml (2floz) vegetable oil*	50ml (2floz) dry white wine
Salt to taste	

Soak the bread in the wine, then squeeze out dry.

Put the meat through a mincer 3 times, add the bread and put through the mincer once more. Add all the other ingredients and knead for 10 minutes. Wet palms of the hands with the leftover wine and shape the meat mixture into small balls.

Heat the oil to sizzling point and put in the balls. Reduce the heat to very low and cook until both sides are well-browned. This should take 25–30 minutes.

The cooked köfte (with a crusty shell but succulent core) should be placed on absorbant paper to remove excess oil before serving. Serve hot with a border of plain pilav. An accompaniment of tomato salad and vinaigrette dressing, together with a diced cucumber, crushed garlic and natural yogurt sauce rapidly whisked and chilled (Cacik), cleanses the palate.

*Personal experience suggests that the best results are obtained with 1.5 litres (2¾ pints) of vegetable oil heated to the required temperature in an open wok (AO).

Turkish cooking

Lady's Thigh Kofte

Kadin Budu Köfte

450g (1lb) lamb
25g (1oz) long-grain rice
50g (2oz) butter
1 teaspoon white pepper
1 teaspoon salt
A little whipped cream

1 onion, chopped
25g (1oz) cream cheese
3 eggs
125ml (4floz) dry sherry
Sprigs of parsley

Fry the onion in the butter until transparent but not brown. Add the sherry, salt and rice, cover and cook until the rice is tender. Remove from the heat. Put the meat 3 times through the mincer then transfer to a heavy based saucepan and cook over a low heat until all the meat juice is extracted. Remove from the heat and add all the other ingredients, including the cooked rice, and knead together for 5 minutes. Shape the mixture into slightly flattened ovals (to resemble a thigh), roll in beaten egg and fry in butter until well-browned. Serve garnished with the parsley and a rosette of whipped cream with a plain pilâv accompaniment.

Kofte on a Skewer

Sis Köftesi

450g (1lb) minced lamb, uncooked
2 eggs
¼ teaspoon finely chopped fresh
   thyme

1 teaspoon garlic salt
Juice of 1 large onion
¼ teaspoon white pepper
30ml (1floz) olive oil

Mix all the ingredients well together (except the olive oil) and knead thoroughly. Grease the palms of the hands with the oil and shape the meat mixture into small sausages. Brush well with oil, thread carefully onto the skewer and grill for 6 minutes, turning continuously.

    Serve with plain pilâv garnished with chopped chives.

Turkish cooking

Kofte in Tomato Purée

Domates Salcali Köfte

450g (1lb) lamb
1 large onion, minced
2 slices thick stale bread
2 eggs
6 sprigs parsley
125ml (4floz) cider

1 teaspoon paprika
75g (3oz) butter
3 large tomatoes, skinned
100g (4oz) plain flour
1 teaspoon salt
Almond oil

Soak the bread in a little cider for 5 minutes, then squeeze out dry. Into a mixing bowl put the meat, onion, bread, parsley, eggs, paprika and salt and knead well together for about 10 minutes. Oil the palms of the hands with almond oil and shape the meat mixture into small, flattened balls. Flour both sides.

Melt the butter and drop in the balls and cook until nicely browned over a low heat.

Add the chopped tomatoes and the remaining cider and heat through. Transfer to the oven and bake for 30–35 minutes at 190°C/375°F/Gas 5. Serve immediately with tomato pilâv.

Casserole of Lamb

Kuzu Güvec

900g (2lb) shoulder of lamb
50g (2oz) butter
3 large potatoes, sliced thickly
3 tomatoes, skinned and cut up
9 spring onions, chopped
1 pimento, chopped
1 teaspoons chopped fresh sorrel
6–7 nasturtium flowers

3 cloves of garlic
1 lettuce, shredded
4 tablespoons chopped fresh dill
2 onions, sliced thickly
1 bay leaf
125ml (4floz) red wine
Salt and pepper

Cut the meat into fairly large pieces and place in an earthenware casserole dish, with all the ingredients, except the nasturtium flowers. Cover with greaseproof paper before putting on the lid. Cook at 190°C/375°F/Gas 5 for 2½–3 hours.

Serve garnished with the nasturtium flowers.

Turkish cooking

Lamb Chops

Kuzu Pirzolasi Pane

6 lamb chops
25g (1oz) plain flour
1 teaspoon pepper
3 tablespoons clarified dripping
3 teaspoons paprika
½ teaspoon olive oil
1 large egg

75g (3oz) toasted crumbs
90ml (3floz) olive oil
75g (3oz) butter
1 teaspoon chopped fresh thyme
Salt to taste
Sprigs of parsley

Trim and clean the fat from the chops and beat with an iron mallet until they are 6mm (¼in) in thickness.

Have prepared in separate plates the flour, breadcrumbs and the egg, which should be beaten very lightly then mixed well with salt, pepper, thyme and the ½ teaspoon of olive oil.

Lightly flour both sides of the chops, dip in the egg mixture and coat with toasted crumbs. Heat the olive oil in a pan and when sizzling put in the chops and fry until golden brown, about 5–6 minutes each side. Do not overcrowd the chops in the pan.

Just before serving pour hot melted butter mixed with the paprika over them.

Garnish with young spring onions and a few sprigs of parsley. Serve with plain or almond pilâv.

Lamb in the Oven

Kuzu Firin

900g (2lb) leg of lamb
125ml (4floz) dry white wine
125ml (4floz) single cream
65g (2½oz) butter
1 egg yolk, small
Salt and pepper

25g (1oz) plain flour
125ml (4floz) milk
6 large potatoes
2 eggs
75g (3oz) grated Gruyère cheese

Put the meat in a tin, pour wine over it and cook at 190°C/375°F/Gas 5 for about 1 hour, or until nicely cooked, basting occasionally with the wine.

Boil the potatoes, skin and slice two of them and lay on a large meat tray. Mash the rest of the potatoes, add the eggs and egg yolk, 25g (1oz) of the butter, 25g (1oz) of the cheese and salt and pepper. Put through a forcing bag and pipe into rosettes around the edge of the meat tray. Keep hot until the meat is cooked.

Slice the meat and arrange it over the sliced potatoes in the tray.

Melt the rest of the butter, add the flour and cook for 2 minutes over a low heat without browning. Add the milk gradually, then the cream, stirring continuously until nicely thickened. Add the rest of the cheese and cook for 3 minutes more. Pour this sauce over the sliced lamb and put the tray under the grill. Cook until the top is delicately browned and serve at once with oriental pilâv.

Turkish cooking

Lamb with Pilaw

Kuzulu Pilâv

450g (1lb) minced lamb
25g (3oz) fresh orange peel
Salt and pepper

25g (1oz) butter
3 tablespoons finely chopped walnuts
1 teaspoon ground allspice

Brown the mince with the butter in a heavy based saucepan. Add the orange peel, walnuts and seasoning, mix well and cook over a low heat until the meat is very tender, about 25–30 minutes.

Pile in the centre of a hot dish and surround with a ring of plain pilâv. Dust with allspice and serve at once.

Albanian Liver

Arnavut Cigeri

450g (1lb) lamb's liver
50g (2oz) plain flour
2 teaspoons paprika
Garlic salt

2 large onions
6 sprigs chopped fresh parsley
225ml (8floz) olive oil

Clean, trim and slice the liver into very small pieces (the size of a walnut) and wash under running water. Put into a bowl with half the paprika and mix well. Roll each piece in flour, then toss in a sieve to shake off the surplus flour. Heat the oil until sizzling and fry the pieces of liver for 1 minute only. Put aside.

Put 2 tablespoons of the hot oil in a separate pan, add the rest of the paprika, stir well and pour over the liver.

Serve cold with thinly sliced raw onions mixed with chopped fresh parsley.

Note: To serve Spanish onions raw, slice thinly and sprinkle with salt. Leave aside for 30 minutes. Squeeze the slices of the onion and salt together until the onions feel limp, then rinse several times under cold running water. Onions prepared in this way leave no unpleasant smell and are digested easily.

Turkish cooking

Mutton Ragout

Koyun

900g (2lb) lamb	600ml (1 pint) chicken stock
75g (3oz) butter	225ml (8floz) cider
60 button onions	4 tablespoons chopped fresh dill
2 pimentos	Salt to taste

Cut the meat into small pieces. Melt the butter in a heavy based saucepan and when just sizzling add the meat. Cook slowly, turning occasionally for 15–20 minutes. Add the onions, the cut up pimentos, salt and two thirds of the stock. Cook gently on a low heat for 2 ½ hours, adding the remaining stock at the end of the first 30 minutes and the cider 45 minutes before the cooking time is finished. Remove the pieces of meat and reduce the liquid to half by rapid boiling. Add the dill and pour over the pieces of meat. Serve immediately.

Ox Tongue

Sigir Dili

1 ox tongue
3 sticks celery
2 carrots, diced
2 tomatoes, skinned and seeded
½ teaspoon chopped fresh basil
225ml (8floz) red wine

1.7 litres (3 pints)
3 chopped onions
90ml (3floz) vegetable oil
1 teaspoon chopped fresh rosemary
5 peppercorns
1 teaspoon garlic salt

Clean and wash the tongue and put into a heavy based saucepan with the water, carrots, cclery, 1 onion, salt and pepper and cook very gently for 1¾ hours, skimming when necessary. Remove the tongue and skin it.

Heat the oil and fry the tongue for 15 minutes. Add the rest of the onions, the rosemary, basil and peppercorns and fry for 15 minutes more. Add the tomatoes and cook for another 5 minutes. Add the wine and 600ml (1 pint) of the strained liquid in which the tongue was cooked. Cover with a napkin and cook for 2 more hours on a very low heat.

Remove the tongue, cool slightly and slice. Sieve the remaining liquid, return to the saucepan and boil uncovered until a thick purée is obtained. Pour this over the sliced tongue and serve hot with piped rosettes of potato purée.

Turkish cooking

Palace Curry

Saray Biftek

900g (2lb) best fillet of steak,
    or lamb
3 cloves garlic
Sliced root ginger the size of a
    large walnut
2 tablespoons curry powder
3 tablespoons redcurrant jelly
1 tablespoon grated fresh coconut
1½ teaspoons salt
2 tablespoons sour apples,
    finely chopped

1 tablespoon dates, finely chopped
2 large onions
3 chillis, chopped
50ml (2floz) vegetable oil
1 tablespoon curry paste
225ml (8floz) vegetable stock
125ml (4floz) coconut milk
Juice of 1 small lemon
2 tablespoons seedless raisins
⅛ teaspoon dry mustard

To make coconut milk:

Grate half a medium-sized coconut and put in a bowl with 225ml (8floz)
boiling water. Cover and leave for 4 hours, then strain before using.

To make the curry:

Heat the oil in a large heavy based saucepan, slice the onions and the garlic
very thinly and fry without browning for 5–6 minutes. Add the chillis and the
meat, cut into cubes. Brown a little, about 3 minutes, then stir in the curry
powder, the paste and the ginger. Stir well and cook for 2 minutes. Add the
grated coconut, coconut milk, stock, redcurrant jelly, apples, raisins and
dates. Cover and simmer very gently for about 2 hours or until the meat is
very tender. Just before the cooking time is over add lemon juice and salt.
Serve hot with plain boiled rice and pickled limes.

Meat and Poultry
Et ve Tavuklar

Rabbit Escallopes

Tavsan

2 large slices of back of rabbit,
   boned and beaten into escallops
1 teaspoon garlic salt
75g (3oz) butter
Slices of thin cheese, Gruyère
   or Cheddar

Toasted breadcrumbs
50ml (2floz) red wine
1 teaspoon chopped fresh rosemary
25g (1oz) plain flour
Beaten egg

Marinate the boned and beaten rabbit slices in the wine, salt and rosemary for 6 hours, turning at the end of 3 hours. Drain well. Roll in beaten egg and breadcrumbs and sauté in the butter for 9–10 minutes, then remove from the butter and keep hot.

   Add the flour to the butter left in the pan and stir until bubbly. Cook for 2–3 minutes, stirring all the time. Add the wine mixture in which the rabbit marinated and stir until smooth.

   Place a thin slice of cheese on each escallop of rabbit and grill until the cheese is a golden brown. Arrange on a serving dish and pour the wine sauce over the escallops. Serve at once with plain pilâv.

Turkish cooking

Stuffing No.1 for Tomatoes or Green Peppers

225g (8oz) minced beef, or lamb
50g (2oz) long-grain rice
125ml (4floz) vegetable stock
2 tablespoons chopped fresh dill
Salt

30ml (1floz) vegetable oil
30ml (1floz) red wine
1 onion, finely chopped
½ teaspoon white pepper
1 teaspoon chopped fresh parsley

Heat the oil and fry the onions until lightly browned. Add the rice and stock and cook until the rice is soft and all the liquid has been absorbed, about 10–12 minutes. Remove from the heat and cool slightly. Add the minced beef, or lamb, wine, dill, parsley, pepper and salt and knead for 5 minutes. This stuffing is now ready to be used.

Note: This stuffing is to be used with dishes that are served hot.

Stuffed Turkey

Hindi Dolmasi

1 young turkey, 1.8–2.7kg (4–6lb)
225ml (8floz) water
3 onions, chopped finely
2 cloves garlic
6 sprigs of dill chopped fresh
1 tablespoon blackcurrants
Salt to taste
A little chicken stock

225g (8oz) long-grain rice
100g (4oz) butter
2 carrots, cut into quarters
1 large tomato, skinned and chopped
1 tablespoon pine kernels
½ teaspoon pepper
½ teaspoon chopped fresh basil
1 tablespoon red wine

Put the cleaned turkey into a large saucepan with the water, half of the butter, onions, carrots and garlic, cover and bring to the boil. Remove from the heat and put the saucepan into a hot oven (230°C/450°F/Gas 8). Keep the cover on and baste occasionally, cooking until the turkey is tender. For the last 10 minutes remove the cover, baste and allow the bird to brown. Remove from the oven, put the bird in a warm place and strain the fat and juice in the saucepan. Increase the amount to 450ml (¾ pint) of liquid by adding stock and 1 tablespoon of red wine. Put this liquor aside as it will be used for the making of the rice stuffing.

In the meantime, cut up the liver of the turkey into small pieces, sauté for 3 minutes in butter and leave aside to keep hot. Clean the rice and cover with almost boiling water and leave aside to get cold. Wash several times under running water and drain.

Melt half the remainder of the butter, add 1 more onion finely chopped, add the pine kernels and fry until both are nicely browned. Add the rice and cook for another 8–10 minutes on medium heat. Add the liquor (left aside from the turkey), the blackcurrants, tomatoes, herbs and seasoning, cover and cook on a slightly reduced heat until all the liquid has been absorbed by the rice, about another 12–15 minutes. Add the dill and the liver, stir well and remove from the heat. Stuff the turkey tightly with this mixture, place in a warm oven (190°C/375°F/Gas 5) for 40 minutes, then serve at once.

Turkish cooking

Pressed Veal

Dana Rosto

900g (2lb) side of veal
⅛ teaspoon sugar
⅛ teaspoon salt
⅛ teaspoon paprika
¼ teaspoon dry mustard

⅛ teaspoon white pepper
30ml (1floz) lemon juice
50ml (2floz) olive oil
2 cloves crushed garlic

Pound the veal with a heavy mallet as thinly as possible and marinate in the above ingredients for 3 hours, turning every 20 minutes. Drain well and spread out flat. Sprinkle with:

1 onion, minced
1 teaspoon allspice

Salt and pepper to taste

Roll up tightly, sew up the ends with strong thread and tie in two or three places with string. Put the meat in a deep saucepan of boiling water, adding:

1 onion, coarsely chopped
1 bay leaf

1 stalk green celery

Simmer for 2–2¼ hours or until the meat is very tender. Remove from the water, drain and press into a long tin. Cover with a napkin and a very heavy weight until it is cold.
   Serve cut into slices with plain salad.

Veal Steak

Dana Tavasi

450g (1lb) veal steak
175g (6oz) tomatoes, skinned
   and chopped
1 teaspoon salt
2 onions, finely chopped
1 teaspoon chopped fresh chervil
40g (1½oz) mushrooms, diced and
   sautéed in butter for 3 minutes

65g (2½oz) butter
1 bayleaf
1 teaspoon white pepper
1 leaf of rosemary
50ml (2floz) double cream
40g (1½oz) buttered crumbs

Melt the butter and brown the veal steak (which should be cut into cubes).

Add the tomatoes, salt and pepper, bayleaf, onion, rosemary and chervil and simmer until the meat is very tender, about 55 minutes.

Turn the whole thing into a baking dish, add the cream, mushrooms and buttered crumbs and cook at 190°C/375°F/Gas 5 for 15–20 minutes.

Finish off by browning the crumbs under the grill and serve immediately.

Turkish cooking

Veal Steak with Wine

Sarapli Dana

4 pieces of veal steak, 2.5cm
  (1in) thick
50ml (2floz) chicken stock
50g (2oz) butter

Seasoned flour, 25g (1oz) plain
  flour, 1 teaspoon garlic salt,
  1 teaspoon paprika, sifted together
125ml (4floz) dry white wine

Pound the steaks until the fibre is well separated and the steaks are very thin.
Season with salt and pepper and pour half the wine over them. Marinate for
3 hours, turning after 1½ hours. Drain but do not dry and dip each steak in
the seasoned flour. Brown both sides in butter over a fierce heat. This is for
the purpose of sealing the meat juices and should be done very speedily.

Remove from the heat when nicely sealed, add the stock and the
remaining wine, cover and cook very slowly until tender.

Serve in its own juice with a border of white pilâv cooked in veal or
chicken stock.

Stuffed Breast of Veal

Dana Gögüs Dolmasi

900g (2lb) breast of veal, boned
2 chopped shallots
2 beaten egg yolks
1 teaspoon chopped fresh chives
450ml (¾ pint) chicken stock
Salt and pepper

2 slices stale bread, soaked in
    chicken stock
150g (5oz) chopped mushrooms
40g (1½oz) butter
1 teaspoon chopped fresh dill
1 large onion, minced

Pound the meat to half its original thickness.

Mix the bread, shallots and mushrooms, add the egg yolks and the seasonings. Mix well and spread over the veal as evenly as possible. Roll and skewer tightly.

Melt the butter, add the veal and the minced onion and cook until the meat is well-browned all over. Add the stock and herbs, cover and simmer until the meat is tender, about 2¼ hours.

Serve hot in its own juices.

Turkish cooking

Hot Vegetable Dishes
Sicak Sebze Yemekleri

Aubergine Casserole

Oturtma

3 large fresh aubergines
125ml (4floz) vegetable stock
1 large onion, finely chopped
½ teaspoon white pepper

90ml (3floz) vegetable oil
100g (4oz) minced lamb, uncooked
3 tomatoes, skinned and chopped
½ teaspoon salt

Fry the onions in a third of the oil until transparent but not brown. Add the meat and cook for a further 10 minutes. Add one of the tomatoes and cook for another 10 minutes. Add salt and pepper, stir, and remove from the heat.

Cut off the tops of the aubergines and pare off the skin 1cm (½in) strips lengthways. Cut the aubergines in two, lengthways, salt generously and leave aside for 30 minutes until all the bitter juice of the vegetable has been extracted. Wash thoroughly under running water and fry in the remaining oil until nicely browned on both sides.

Arrange the pieces side by side in a wide-bottomed pan, cut side upwards, and spread with the mince mixture. Arrange slices of tomato on top, add the stock, cover and cook on a medium heat for 30–40 minutes.

Serve hot in their own juice with a plain or tomato pilâv.

Turkish cooking

Aubergine

Patlican Karniyarik

4 aubergines
225ml (8floz) vegetable oil
3 small onions, chopped
4 green peppers
Salt to taste

225g (8oz) minced beef, or lamb
225ml (8floz) vegetable stock
3 tomatoes, skinned and halved
½ teaspoon pepper

Fry the onions in 30ml (1floz) of the oil until transparent but not brown. Add the mince and cook for another 10 minutes. Add two of the tomatoes and the seasoning and cook until the tomatoes are a purée. Remove from the heat. Prepare the aubergines in the same way as for Imam Bayildi (page 103) but before filling them fry them in the rest of the oil until they are a very pale brown. Remove very carefully and lay them in a wide-bottomed saucepan, side by side. Fill the cut parts with the minced beef or lamb mixture and put a slice of tomato on the centre of each and thin strips of the green pepper on each end. Add the stock and cook over a low heat for 40–45 minutes. Dish up very carefully without breaking the aubergines.

Note: This dish is served as a main dish with plain pilâv to follow, and salad.

Aubergine Kebab

Patlican Kebabi

450g (1lb) leg of lamb
2 tomatoes, skinned
175ml (6floz) dry white wine
Salt and pepper

50g (2oz) butter
225ml (8floz) water
1 large onion
2 large aubergines

The aubergines should be smooth and shiny, quite unwithered looking and of a dark purplish colour. Peel them lengthways in strips, leaving a line of flesh between each section of purple skin. Cut into 2.5cm (1in) thick slices and put into a bowl, sprinkling generously with salt, and leave aside for 30 minutes. This must be done with all aubergines in order that the bitter juice may be extracted. Wash several times under running cold water, dry in a napkin and plunge into the sizzling butter. Cook until both sides are nicely browned then remove with a draining spoon and put on one side.

Cut the meat into small cubes and sauté in the same butter, 2 minutes for each side. As each pan of meat is cooked transfer it to a larger heavy based saucepan which should be warming by the side of the cooker.

Peel the onion and cut into thin slices, cut the tomatoes and fry in the butter mixture (the meat will have left some of its own juice). Cook for 3 minutes, then add to the meat in the saucepan. Add the cooked slices of aubergine last of all and the salt and pepper to taste. Cover and cook on a very gentle heat for 2–2½ hours. *Do not* stir but shake the pan occasionally. At the end of the first hour add the wine. Serve hot with plain pilâv.

Turkish cooking

Aubergine Mousaka

Patlican Musakkasi

450g (1lb) minced beef, or lamb
6 aubergines
3 tablespoons finely chopped onion
½ teaspoon chopped fresh sorrel
125ml (4floz) milk
75g (3oz) grated Cheddar cheese
Salt and pepper
4 large tomatoes, skinned and
　chopped

50g (2oz) butter
½ tablespoon finely chopped fresh
　parsley
25g (1oz) plain flour
125ml (4floz) vegetable stock
Butter for frying
40g (1½oz) buttered crumbs

Melt half the butter and fry the onion for 3 minutes. Add the mince and cook until all the meat juice has been extracted and then absorbed again, about 20 minutes. Add the tomatoes and stock. Season, cover and simmer until the meat is tender, about 30 minutes. Add the parsley and remove from the heat. Melt the rest of the butter, add the flour and cook without browning for 3 minutes. Add the milk gradually, stirring all the time, bring to boiling point and then add the cheese and simmer for 10 minutes, stirring to prevent any lumps.

Cut off stalks of aubergines, pare the dark outer skin lengthways leaving strips 1cm (½in) apart, and cut the vegetable into thick slices. Salt generously and leave aside to extract the bitter juices. After 30 minutes wash well and drain. Pat dry and cook in butter until each slice is golden brown then drain on paper.

Grease a baking dish and arrange layers of meat and aubergine over it, finishing with a layer of aubergine. Pour over the cheese sauce, sprinkle with a little more cheese and the buttered breadcrumbs and brown in a hot oven (230°C/450°F/Gas 8). Serve hot with plain pilâv.

Aubergine Sauce

Patlican Salçasi

3 fresh aubergines
40g (1½oz) butter
300ml (½ pint) single cream
¼ teaspoon chopped fresh chives

40g (1½oz) plain flour
40g (1½oz) grated Cheddar cheese
Salt to taste
½ teaspoon lemon rind

Melt the butter and cook the flour for 3 minutes over a low heat without browning, and stirring all the time. Leave aside. Add the salt, chives etc.

Grill the unpeeled aubergines over a fierce heat and then peel off the burned skin which should flake off very easily. Cut the pulp into small pieces, add to the butter and flour and mash thoroughly. Return to a moderate heat, add the cream gradually and stir until the mixture is completely free from lumps. Add the cheese and stir again until quite smooth and velvety.

This sauce should be served hot with roast chicken.

Turkish cooking

Aubergine With White Cheese

Peynirli Patlican

3 aubergines
4 large eggs
1 tablespoon chopped fresh dill
75g (3oz) toasted breadcrumbs
225ml (8floz) olive oil for frying

225g (8oz) cream cheese
2 tablespoons chopped fresh parsley
1 teaspoon chopped fresh chives
½ teaspoon garlic salt

Remove the tops of the aubergines and peel the skins in 1cm (1/2in) wide strips lengthways. Cut the aubergines into quarters, lengthways and leave aside for 30 minutes, sprinkled generously with salt. Wash well, dry and fry in olive oil until pale brown. Leave aside to cool.

Mash the cheese with a fork, add the salt, parsley, dill, chives and half the eggs and mix well together. Spread this mixture over half the aubergines, cut sides upwards, and arrange the other half of the aubergines on top, sandwich fashion.

Beat the other two eggs lightly and roll the aubergine sandwiches in this and then in the toasted crumbs. Fry in olive oil for 6–7 minutes and serve hot.

Broad Beans and Lamb

Kuzulu Bakla

900g (2lb) fresh broad beans	65g (2½oz) butter
350g (12oz) boned lamb	2 onions, chopped
1 tablespoon chopped fresh chervil	450ml (¾ pint) chicken stock
Juice of 1 small lemon	2 teaspoons sugar
Salt to taste	1 teaspoon crushed pine kernels

Cut the meat into small pieces and put with the butter, onions, chervil, pine kernels and salt. Cover and cook for 30 minutes, shaking the pan occasionally. Remove from the heat and leave aside.

String the beans, wash and drain and mix with the lemon juice and add to the meat mixture. Add the stock and sugar, cover with greaseproof paper sprinkled with water, put on the lid and cook for 1½–2 hours until the beans are very tender.

Serve hot in its own liquor.

Turkish cooking

Stuffed Cabbage Leaves

Etli Lahana Dolmasi

450g (1lb) white cabbage	50ml (2floz) vegetable oil
50g (2oz) long-grain rice	225ml (8floz) water
450g (1lb) minced beef, or lamb	2 large onions
1 tablespoon tomato ketchup	1 teaspoon pepper
1 teaspoon salt	225ml (8floz) vegetable stock

Cut cabbage in half, lengthways and take out the tender middle part (this can be used grated for salads). Wash the remaining cabbage and put into boiling salted water and cook for 2 minutes. Strain off the water and allow the cabbage to cool. Tear off the leaves gently and cut into 10cm (4in) squares. Melt half the oil in a pan, add the onions (finely chopped) and fry until pale brown. Add the cleaned rice and the stock and cook over a moderate heat until the rice is tender, about 10–12 minutes. Remove from the heat, add the mince and seasoning and knead together for 5 minutes.

Take 1 teaspoon of this mixture and put on the centre of a square of cabbage, fold envelope fashion, bottom, top and sides, and arrange at the bottom of a shallow, wide-based saucepan. Continue until all the cabbage and filling has been used. Add the tomato ketchup and the rest of the oil and pour on 125ml (4floz) of boiling water. Cover the saucepan with a plate with a heavy weight over it and cook for 35 minutes on a moderate heat. Serve hot.

Cabbage With Lamb

Kuzulu Lahana

900g (2lb) cabbage
50g (2oz) butter
450ml (¾ pint) vegetable stock
Salt and pepper

450g (1lb) lamb
2 large onions, chopped finely
2 pimentos, cut into strips

Melt the butter, add the onions and the lamb cut into small cubes, cover and cook for 25 minutes, shaking the pan frequently to prevent sticking.

Clean the cabbage, discarding the tough outer leaves and cut into small pieces. Add to the meat and onions. Add salt and pepper and the pimento strips, cover and cook for another 15 minutes, still shaking the pan occasionally.

Add the stock, cover, and continue cooking on a very reduced heat for 2¼ hours.

Serve hot in its own juice.

Turkish cooking

French Beans with Meat

Etli Taze Fasulye

900g (2lb) French beans
2 large onions, chopped
2 tomatoes, skinned and seeded
1 teaspoon salt
50ml (2floz) vegetable oil

700g (1½lb) lamb or veal (with a little fat left on)
1.2 litres (2 pints) chicken stock
1 teaspoon chopped fresh rosemary

Cut the meat into small pieces. Heat the oil and fry the onions for 5 minutes. Add the meat and cook for another 15 minutes on a moderate heat. Add the tomatoes, cut up, the stock, rosemary and salt. Cover tightly and cook for about 1 hour on a low heat.

String and wash the beans and cut into strips. Add to the pan and continue cooking until the beans are very tender. Serve hot in its own liquor with plain pilâv.

Haricot Beans With Lamb

Etli Kuru Fasulye

225g (8oz) haricot beans, small	*65g (2½oz) butter*
2 tomatoes, skinned and chopped	*1 pimento, sliced*
225g (8oz) fatty lamb	*2 onions, chopped finely*
600ml (1 pint) chicken stock	*Salt and pepper*
½ teaspoon chopped fresh thyme	*½ teaspoon chopped fresh basil*

Soak the beans overnight in slightly salted water, strain and wash well. Put into boiling water and cook for 25 minutes. Strain and leave aside.

Melt the butter and fry the onions until transparent, then add the meat cut into small pieces and cook for another 15 minutes, shaking the pan occasionally to prevent sticking. Add the chopped tomatoes and pimento strips, seasoning, herbs and stock, cover and cook on a low heat for 45 minutes. Add the haricot beans and the water in which they were cooked, and cook until the beans are very tender but unbroken.

Should any more liquid be necessary (in case the beans are old and take too long to cook) then add more hot water.

Serve hot with plain pilâv.

Turkish cooking

Leeks With Mutton

Etli Pirasa

900g (2lb) leeks
40g (1½oz) butter
1 large onion, chopped
2 large tomatoes, skinned

450g (1lb) lamb
3 tablespoons chopped fresh
    rosemary
225ml (8floz) chicken stock
Salt and pepper

Cut the meat into cubes. Melt half the butter and add the onions and the meat. Cover and cook for 25 minutes, shaking the pan occasionally to prevent burning. Add seasoning, sliced tomatoes and half of the stock, cover and cook on a moderate heat for another 45 minutes. Remove from the heat and leave aside.

In a separate heavy based saucepan melt the rest of the butter and add the washed, white part of the leek, cut into 1cm (½in) slices. Add the rest of the stock, cover and cook on a moderate heat for 20 minutes.

Add the leeks and liquor to the other pan of meat mixture and cook, covered, until the meat is tender, about 50 minutes on a moderate heat.

Serve hot in its own juice, sprinkled with the rosemary.

Marrow With Chicken

Tavuklu Kabak

3 young marrows
600ml (1 pint) water
40g (1½oz) plain flour
225ml (8floz) single cream
50g (2oz) grated Parmesan cheese
900g (2lb) spring chicken

225ml (8floz) dry white wine
40g (1½oz) butter
225ml (8floz) chicken stock
½ teaspoon white pepper
½ teaspoon salt

Put the cleaned chicken into a heavy based saucepan with the water, wine and salt and simmer gently for 2 hours, removing any scum as it rises to the top. Remove the chicken and by rapid, uncovered boiling reduce the liquor to about 225ml (8floz). Shred the chicken finely and leave aside.

Clean and scrape the marrows, cut in half lengthways and remove all seeds. Leave in salt water for 10 minutes. Drain, cover with fresh water and boil for about 35–40 minutes. Remove, drain, and arrange on a lightly greased baking dish, and cut parts uppermost.

Fry the flour in the butter over a low heat for 2–3 minutes. Add the reduced chicken stock gradually, stirring all the time, add the cream and bring to the boil very slowly. Add seasoning and half the cheese and cook for a further 10 minutes without browning. Pour half of this sauce over the shredded chicken and combine well. Spread the mixture over the marrows, pour on the rest of the sauce, add the remaining cheese and bake in a hot oven (230°C/450°F/Gas 8) for about 15 minutes until the top is nicely browned. Serve hot with plain pilâv.

Turkish cooking

Stuffed Marrows

Kabak Dolmasi

3 young marrows
350g (12oz) minced lamb
1 teaspoon sweet marjoram
3 tomatoes, skinned and seeded
50g (2oz) long-grain rice
½ tablespoon chopped fresh chervil
Salt to taste

900ml (1½ pints) vegetable stock
50ml (2floz) vegetable oil
1 teaspoon white pepper
1 onion, chopped
2 tablespoons chopped fresh parsley
125ml (4floz) dry white wine

Select fat young marrows. Scrape and cut off the bottom end. Scoop out the insides, discard seeds, and cover the marrows with water and lemon juice and leave aside.

Put half the oil in a pan and cook the onions until transparent. Add the wine and the cleaned rice, cover the saucepan and cook for 10 minutes. Remove from the heat and add the lamb, salt, parsley, sweet marjoram, chervil and salt and pepper and cook for 5–7 minutes. Add the marrow pulp to this and remove from the heat.

Drain and wipe the marrows and stuff tightly with the meat mixture and place in a large saucepan. Add the rest of the oil, an eighth of the stock, cover tightly and cook for 15 minutes on a medium heat. Add the cut up tomatoes and the rest of the stock and cook for another hour. Serve hot in their own liquor, decorated with dill.

Young Marrows

Taze Kabak

2 young marrows
50g (2oz) butter
1 onion, chopped
½ tablespoon chopped fresh dill
1 teaspoon paprika

225g (8oz) veal
450ml (¾ pint) vegetable stock
3 tomatoes, skinned and seeded
½ tablespoon chopped fresh tarragon
A little garlic salt

Cut the meat into small pieces, salt, add the dill and tarragon and leave aside for 1 hour, turning at the end of 30 minutes.

Melt half the butter in a heavy based saucepan, add the onions and meat and cook over a low heat for 30 minutes, shaking the pan occasionally. Add the cut up tomatoes and cook for another 10 minutes, then remove from the heat and leave aside.

Scrape and clean the marrows, cutting off each end. Cut into four, lengthways, and remove the seeds. Cut into cubes of about 25cm (1in).

Put these into a pan with the rest of the butter and a quarter of the stock and cook on a medium heat for 10 minutes.

Put the meat and marrows into a tray in layers making sure that the top layer is of marrows. Add the rest of the hot stock and the liquor left from the meat and marrow saucepans and cover with greaseproof paper sprinkled with water. Cover and cook on a medium heat until the marrows are tender, about 1 hour, depending on the age of the marrows.

Serve hot with plain pilâv, in its own juice and garnished with dill and tarragon and sprinkled with paprika.

Turkish cooking

Okra with Breast of Duck

Ördekli Bamya

700g (1½lb) okra
450ml (¾pint) chicken stock
3 large onions, chopped
1 green pepper, sliced and seeded
225ml (8floz) tarragon vinegar
1 large orange, sliced

900g (2lb) cooked breast of duck
30ml (1floz) vegetable oil
3 large tomatoes, skinned and
  seeded
6 mushrooms, sliced
125ml (4floz) red wine
Salt and pepper

Cut the breast of duck into slices.

Heat the oil and sauté the onions for 5 minutes, add the mushrooms and cook for another 5 minutes. Add a quarter of the stock and the slices of duck and bring to boiling point very slowly. Remove from the heat.

Cut the bottoms and tops off the okra and wash well under running water. Put in a bowl, add vinegar and 2 tablespoons salt. Mix together well and leave for 1 hour. Wash and drain several times, arrange in a dish, with the tomatoes (one layer okra, one layer tomatoes etc, with the meat mixture as the middle layer and finishing with a layer of okra). Add the green pepper, the orange slices and salt and pepper, the wine and the rest of the stock. Cover and bring to the boil, reduce the heat to low medium and cook for 1¼ hours. During the last 10 minutes cook uncovered at a higher temperature so that the liquor is reduced and thickened. Serve hot in its own juice.

Peas With Lamb

Kuzulu Bezelye

900g (2lb) shelled peas	*50ml (2floz) vegetable oil*
450g (1lb) boned lamb	*2 small onions, chopped*
2 tablespoons chopped fresh dill	*1 teaspoon chopped fresh sorrel*
½ teaspoon chopped fresh thyme	*½ tablespoon sugar*
600ml (1 pint) vegetable stock	*½ teaspoon celery salt*

Cut the meat into small pieces. Melt the oil, add the onions, meat, thyme, sorrel, half of the dill and the salt. Cover and cook for 30 minutes, shaking the pan now and again to prevent burning. Add the stock and bring to the boil, skimming as necessary. Add sugar and peas and simmer for 40 minutes or until the peas are very tender but not 'mushy'. In the case of very young peas the cooking time will be considerably reduced.

Add the rest of the dill, stir once and remove from the heat. Serve in own reduced liquor as a main dish, with either plain pilâv or boiled rice.

Turkish cooking

Stuffed Green Peppers

Etli Biber Dolmasi

6 large green peppers
225ml (8floz) vegetable stock
Salt

30ml (1floz) vegetable oil
2 tablespoons chopped fresh parsley

Choose your peppers carefully. They should be medium in size and of a uniform shape, not too intensely green nor too yellow.

Cut out the stalk very carefully, this will act as your 'lid' later on, and be careful not to split the peppers. Clean out all the seeds and wash well under running water. Boil for 5 minutes, then strain this water off, this renders the peppers less bitter. Add fresh boiling water and boil for 5 more minutes. Strain and leave aside to cool.

Fill with Stuffing No. 1 (see page 66), adding the stalk as the cover. Stand upright in a heavy based saucepan, add the stock, oil and salt and cook over a moderate heat for 35–40 minutes. Serve hot in their own liquor and decorated with parsley.

Potatoes and Minced Beef

Kiymali Patates

900g (2lb) potatoes
90ml (3floz) vegetable oil
450ml (¾ pint) vegetable stock
1 green pepper, seeded and cut
  in strips
1 teaspoon garlic salt

225ml (8floz) vegetable oil for
  sautéing
2 large tomatoes, skinned
350g (12oz) minced beef, or lamb
2 onions, chopped
1 teaspoon pepper
75g (3oz) sliced mushrooms

Peel the potatoes, wash them and cut into thickish slices. Leave in salted water.

Heat 90ml (3floz) of vegetable oil and fry the onions for 5 minutes. Add the mushrooms and cook for another 3 minutes. Add the mince, salt and the slices of green pepper and cook for another 15 minutes. Add the chopped tomatoes, remove from the heat and keep warm.

Sauté the potatoes in the oil and when golden brown add to the other ingredients. Pour over the stock and cook on a moderate heat, covered, for 20 minutes.

Serve hot.

Turkish cooking

Stuffed Potatoes

Patates Dolmasi

1.4kg (3lb) large round potatoes
75g (3oz) finely chopped tongue
50g (2oz) butter
125ml (4floz) single cream
Chopped fresh parsley
2 slices cooked chicken breast,
  minced

75g (3oz) sliced button mushrooms,
  sautéed
2 egg yolks
½ teaspoon pepper
½ teaspoon salt

Choose well-shaped potatoes of the same size. Scrape and cut a thin slice off one end of each so that they can stand upright on a dish. Wash, dry and place on a greased baking sheet and bake in a moderate oven (190°C/375°F/Gas5) for about 30 minutes, or until nicely browned. Remove from the oven and cut a 'lid' off the top end of each potato and scoop out the insides, leaving a shell at least 1cm (½in) thick.

Take about a third of the potato insides, add salt and pepper and mash with a fork. Add half the butter, the cream, yolks of eggs, chicken breast, tongue and mushrooms. Mix well and fill the potato shells and put on the covers. Arrange upright on a baking dish, brush with the rest of the butter, melted, and bake for 10 minutes at 230°C/450°F/Gas 8. Just before serving brush once more with melted butter and roll thoroughly in the parsley.

Stuffed Tomatoes

Domates Dolmasi

6 large tomatoes	25g (1oz) butter
225ml (8floz) vegetable stock	6 sprigs parsley
Salt and pepper	

Wash the tomatoes and cut a 'lid' from the top of each. Clean out the pulp inside, taking care not to break the skins. Fill with Stuffing No. 1 (see page 66) and arrange in a shallow pan side by side. Add the stock, butter and seasoning and cook for 30 minutes.

Serve hot with plain pilâv, decorated with finely chopped fresh parsley.

Turkish cooking

Turlu

450g (1lb) veal
900ml (1½ pints) vegetable stock
175g (6oz) okra
175g (6oz) french beans, sliced
350g (12oz) aubergines (sliced
    and left in salt for 30 minutes)
2 tablespoons vinegar

90ml (3floz) vegetable oil
2 large onions, chopped
3 green peppers, seeded and sliced
175g (10oz) marrow, diced
175g (6oz) tomatoes, chopped and
    skinned
Salt

Heat the oil and fry the onions until transparent. Cut the veal into small pieces, add to the onions and fry for a further 20 minutes on a moderate heat, stirring frequently. Remove from the heat and leave aside.

Clean and prepare the okra and put in a bowl with the vinegar and a generous sprinkling of salt and leave for 30 minutes, then rinse thoroughly under running water.

Put the beans and marrow into a heavy based saucepan with 30ml (1floz) of the vegetable oil, add half the stock, cover and cook for 25 minutes, shaking the pan occasionally.

After washing the salt and bitter juice from the aubergines, sauté them in 50ml (2floz) of the vegetable oil for 7 minutes.

Add the okra to the beans and marrows, add the meat and onions, green peppers and half of the tomatoes. Add the aubergines and the rest of the tomatoes and the remaining stock and cook over a moderate heat for 1¼ –1½ hours.

Serve hot in its own reduced liquor with plain pilâv.

Stuffed Vine Leaves

Etli Yaprak Dolmasi

450g (1lb) vine leaves	225ml (8floz) chicken stock
50g (2oz) long-grain rice	225ml (8floz) dry white wine
2 onions, chopped	75g (3oz) sliced mushrooms
450g (1lb) minced lamb	50ml (2floz) vegetable oil
6 sprigs dill	½ teaspoon white pepper
½ teaspoon chopped fresh rosemary	Garlic salt

Put the washed and cleaned vine leaves into boiling water and cook for 5 minutes. Strain, cut off the stalks, and cut each leaf in half down the middle vein.

Heat half the oil and lightly brown the onions, add the mushrooms and cook for a further 3 minutes. Add the stock, the cleaned rice, and cook for 10–12 minutes on a moderate heat until all the liquid has been absorbed by the rice. Remove from the heat, add the lamb, dill, rosemary, pepper and salt and knead for 5 minutes.

With the hairy sides of the leaves facing upwards put one good teaspoon of stuffing on each leaf and roll up fairly tightly, the shiny sides of the leaves facing outwards.

Arrange side by side at the bottom of a shallow pan, layer by layer, and add the rest of the oil and the wine. Cover with a plate with a heavy weight on top, cover and cook over a moderate heat for 35 minutes. Serve hot.

Turkish cooking

Cold Vegetable Dishes
Zeytinyagli Sebzeler

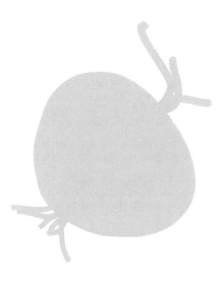

Artichoke

Yer Elmasi

900g (2lb) artichokes
1 lemon
125ml (4floz) water
2 onions, chopped
1 teaspoon garlic salt

225ml (8floz) olive oil
50g (2oz) long-grain rice
3 diced carrots
6 sprigs dill
75g (3oz) tomatoes, sliced and skinned

Heat the oil to boiling point, add the onions and fry until transparent but not brown. Add the tomatoes and cook for another 4 minutes.

Peel the artichokes thinly and slice them. Add these, with the water, to the onions, cover and cook for another 15 minutes, shaking the pan occasionally. Add seasoning and 600ml (1 pint) more of hot water and cook until the artichokes are tender, about 15 minutes.

Boil the rice in a separate pan, drain after 10 minutes and add the rice to the artichokes with lemon juice. Cook for 3 minutes longer, uncovered, and allow to cool in its own juice.

Serve very cold, garnished with the dill.

Turkish cooking

Stuffed Aubergine

Patlican Dolmasi

6 large aubergines
225ml (8floz) water
50ml (2floz) olive oil

Salt to taste
Lemon and chopped fresh parsley

Cut off the stalks of the aubergines and from the other end cut off a 'lid'. Scoop out the insides and leave aside. Put plenty of coarse salt in the cavities and on the outside skins and leave for 30 minutes. Wash several times under cold running water and fill very tightly with Stuffing No. 2 (page 117). Put on the 'lids' and arrange, upright, on a baking dish. Add water and olive oil and salt. Cover and cook on a moderate heat for 1 hour, until the aubergines are soft.

Allow to cool in its own liquor and serve well-chilled with thin slices of lemon and chopped fresh parsley.

Broad Beans

Bakla

900g (2lb) fresh broad beans
125ml (4floz) olive oil
2 teaspoons sugar
Juice of 1 lemon
Salt to taste

450ml (¾ pint) water
2 bunches spring onions
2 tablespoons chopped fresh mint
2 tablespoons chopped fresh dill

String the beans and wash well. Leave them whole and pour the lemon juice over them. Add a sprinkling of salt and leave aside for 15 minutes. Line the bottom of a strong, broad saucepan with a vine leaf and lay on this the biggest beans. Pile the mint, dill and spring onions (these last should be cut to the size of the beans) in the centre and continue filling up with beans. Sprinkle with the sugar and add the water and olive oil. Cover with greaseproof paper sprinkled with water, put on the saucepan lid and cook on a moderate heat for 1½-2 hours until the beans are very tender but unbroken. Do not open the saucepan during the cooking process but shake occasionally to prevent sticking.

Leave to get cold in the saucepan, then serve well-chilled with fresh yogurt in which a clove of garlic has been crushed.

Turkish cooking

Stuffed Cabbage Leaves

Lahana Dolmasi

450g (1lb) white cabbage
Stuffing No.2 (see page 117)

Juice of ½ lemon
225ml (8floz) cold water

Cut the cabbage in half, lengthways, and remove the tender middle part (this can be used in salads). Wash the remaining cabbage and put into boiling salted water and cook for 12 minutes. Strain off the water and allow to cool. Tear off the leaves gently and cut into 10cm (4in) squares.

Put one good-sized teaspoon of Stuffing No. 2 on each square, fold envelope-fashion and arrange at the bottom of a shallow pan which has been lined with cabbage leaves to prevent burning.

Sprinkle on the lemon juice, add the cold water, cover with a heavy plate, put on the pan lid and cook on a medium heat for 1 hour. Allow to cool in its own pan and serve very cold.

French Beans in Olive Oil

Zeytinyagli Taze Fasulya

900g (2lb) French beans	175ml (6floz) olive oil
1 large onion, finely chopped	2 tomatoes, skinned and seeded
1 teaspoon sugar	600ml (1 pint) water
Salt to taste	225ml (8floz) dry white wine

String and wash the beans and cut into long thin strips. Put into a pan with the onions, tomatoes and salt. Add the oil and half the wine. Cover and cook for about 20 minutes on a medium heat, shaking the pan occasionally. Boil the rest of the wine with all the water and add to the beans and cook, covered, until tender. If the beans are old and rather stringy and will not cook with this amount of liquid, add a little more hot water from time to time. Add the sugar last of all, stir carefully, remove from the heat and allow to cool in the pan.

Serve cold in its own liquor.

Turkish cooking

Haricot Beans in Olive Oil

Zeytinyagli Kuru Fasulya

350g (12oz) haricot beans	*300ml (½ pint) olive oil*
1 potato	*2 sticks celery, cut small*
2 carrots, diced	*1 large onion, chopped*
3 cloves garlic	*600ml (1 pint) water*
50ml (2floz) lemon juice	*1 teaspoon sugar*
4 tablespoons chopped fresh parsley	*6 spring onions, chopped*
Salt and pepper	

Soak the beans overnight, strain, wash and put in boiling water. Cook for 30 minutes, then remove from the heat.

Fry the onions in half the olive oil until pale brown, add the water and bring to the boil. Add the celery, potato, carrots, garlic, spring onions, sugar and beans. Cover and cook on a low heat until the beans are tender. Add the rest of the oil, season and cook for another 10 minutes. Add lemon juice and remove from the heat.

Allow to cool in its own liquor and serve cold, sprinkled with chopped fresh parsley and crisp French bread or warmed pitta (pide).

Aubergine

Imam Bayildi

4 aubergines	225ml (8floz) olive oil
4 large onions	4 tomatoes, skinned
12 cloves garlic	12 sprigs parsley
450ml (¾ pint) water	1 teaspoon sugar
Salt to taste	

Cut the onion into thin half-moon slices. Chop the tomatoes and parsley and mix with the onion slices. Add the garlic and salt and leave aside. Leave the stalk on the aubergines but peel the dark outer skin in 1cm (½in) wide strips, lengthways, then make a deep incision in the centre. Sprinkle generously with coarse rock salt and leave aside for 30 minutes to extract the vegetable's bitter juices.

Wash well and pat dry. Take the onion mixture and fill the aubergines with this then lay them side by side in a wide-bottomed saucepan.

Add the water, olive oil, salt and a sprinkling of sugar. Put a plate on them and then cover the saucepan. Cook until the aubergines are soft and tender and the liquor reduced to almost nothing (less than 1 tablespoon should remain in the saucepan), about 1½ hours on a medium heat. Allow to cool in the saucepan and serve very cold.

Turkish cooking

Stuffed Green Peppers

Biber Dolmasi

6 large green peppers
Stuffing No.2 (see page 117)

225ml (8floz) cold water

Choose peppers of equal size. Cut out the stalk carefully, this will act as the 'lid', and clean out all the seeds. Wash well under running water taking care not to split the skins of the peppers. Boil for 5 minutes, then strain this water away, add freshly boiling water and cook for another 5 minutes. Strain and leave aside to cool.

Fill with Stuffing No.2, adding the stalk as a 'lid'.

Stand upright in a wide shallow pan, add the water and cook for 50–55 minutes, at a fairly high heat to begin with and on a medium heat for the last 5 minutes. Keep covered throughout cooking. Leave to cool in the saucepan (there should be scarcely any liquor left) and serve very cold.

Stuffed Tomatoes

Domates Dolmasi

6 large well-shaped tomatoes
Stuffing No.2 (see page 117)

125ml (4floz) cold water

Wash the tomatoes and cut a lid from the top of each. Clean out the insides, taking care not to break the skins. Fill with Stuffing No. 2 and arrange side by side in a shallow pan. Add the water, cover and cook on a high heat for 5 minutes. Reduce the heat and continue cooking for another 45 minutes until all the water has evaporated.

Leave to cool in their own pan and serve cold.

Turkish cooking

Stuffed Vine Leaves

Yaprak Dolmasi

450g (1lb) vine leaves
225ml (8floz) cold water

Juice of ½ lemon
Stuffing No.2 (see page 117)

Put the washed and cleaned vine leaves into boiling water and cook for 5 minutes. Strain, cut off the stalks, and cut each leaf in half down the middle vein. With the hairy sides of the leaves facing upwards put one teaspoon of Stuffing No. 2 on each leaf and roll up fairly tightly, like an envelope as far as possible, the shiny sides of the leaves facing outwards.

Line a shallow pan with large, washed vine leaves (this is to prevent the dolma burning) and arrange the stuffed leaves side by side. Sprinkle with the lemon juice, add the cold water, cover with a heavy plate and then the lid and cook on a medium heat for 1 hour.

Allow to cool in its own pan and serve cold.

Cold Vegetable Dishes
Zeytinyagli Sebzeler

Turkish cooking

Borek and Pilaw
Pilâv ve Börekler

Borek With Cheese

Peynirli Börek

225g (8oz) cream cheese
3 tablespoons chopped fresh
  parsley
15g (½oz) butter

1 egg yolk
2 mushrooms, chopped finely
225g (8oz) puff pastry (see 'Kebab in
  Puff Pastry', pages 43-44)

Sauté the mushrooms in the butter for 4–5 minutes, then leave aside to cool. Mix the parsley, cheese and the egg yolk together and add the mushrooms.

Roll out the puff pastry very thinly, fill with the cheese mixture and cut into half-moon shapes with a pastry cutter. Seal the edges with egg yolk. Grease a baking sheet and put the borek on this 2.5cm (1in) apart. Glaze with beaten egg and bake at 190°C/375°F/Gas 5 until golden brown, about 30 minutes.

Can be served hot or cold.

Turkish cooking

Borek With Chicken

Tavuklu Börek

8–12oz (½–¾lb) puff pastry (see
  'Kebab in Puff Pastry', page 43)
1 egg yolk
125ml (4floz) single cream
1 teaspoon paprika
1 teaspoon chopped fresh chervil

1 breast boiled chicken
15g (½oz) butter
125ml (4floz) milk
25g (1oz) plain flour
2 teaspoons fresh coconut, grated
Salt to taste

Mince the chicken breast very finely.

Melt the butter, add flour and fry for 3–4 minutes, stirring all the time.
Add the milk gradually, still stirring, then the cream. Stir vigorously to prevent
lumps forming. Cook for 2 minutes until smooth and velvety. Add the breast
of chicken, egg yolk, coconut, seasoning and chervil, stir thoroughly and
remove from the heat.

Roll out the pastry very thinly, cut into fancy shapes and fill with the
creamed mixture. Put on a greased baking sheet, 2.5cm (1in) apart, and
cook until golden brown in a moderate oven (190°C/375°F/Gas 5).

Serve hot in a ring of green peas.

Borek With Lamb

Talas Börek

350g (12oz) puff pastry (see
  'Kebab in Puff Pastry', page 43)
450g (1lb) lamb
4 onions, chopped finely
6 sprigs chopped fresh parsley
1 teaspoon chopped fresh thyme

50ml (2floz) dry white wine
25g (1oz) butter
½ tablespoon tomato ketchup
1 teaspoon pepper
1 egg
Salt to taste

Cut the lamb into strips, julienne fashion. Melt the butter, add the meat and one onion and cook for 25 minutes over a moderate heat. Add the tomato ketchup, wine and seasoning, cover and cook over a very low heat for 50 minutes. Add the rest of the onions and cook for another 45 minutes until all the liquid is reduced to a thick purée. During this stage shake the pan frequently to prevent sticking. Add the thyme and parsley, stir once, remove from the heat and allow to cool.

Roll out the pastry very thinly, cut into six pieces and roll each piece until it is as thin as paper. Trim into 17.5cm (7in) squares and fill. Seal all the edges with the yolk of an egg and place on a greased baking dish. Bake at 190°C/375°F/Gas 5 until golden brown.

Serve hot.

Turkish cooking

Borek With Mince

Kiymali Börek

350g (12oz) puff pastry (see
  'Kebab in Puff Pastry', page 43)
2 large onions, chopped finely
½ teaspoon salt
½ teaspoon chopped fresh thyme

⅛ teaspoon mace
225g (8oz) minced beef, or lamb
1 teaspoon white pepper
⅛ teaspoon cinnamon

Put the mince and the onions into a saucepan, without water or fat, and on a very low heat cook for 5–7 minutes, shaking the pan occasionally to prevent sticking. Add the herbs and seasoning, cover and cook, still over a low heat, for about 20 minutes, or until the meat has absorbed its own juice. Remove from the heat and allow to get cold.

Roll out the pastry thinly and cut in half. Grease an oval-shaped pie dish and shape the two pieces of pastry to fit it. Line the dish with pastry, add the filling and cover with the rest of the pastry. Prick a few holes here and there so that the steam can escape and brush the top generously with beaten egg. Cook for about 35 minutes or until the top is golden brown at 230°C/450°F/Gas 8.

Chicken Pilâv

Tavuklu Pilâv

900g (2lb) boiled chicken	450ml (¾ pint) chicken stock
25g (1oz) plain flour	40g (1½oz) grated Parmesan cheese
450g (1lb) long-grain rice	25g (1oz) butter
125ml (4floz) single cream	Salt and white pepper

Separate the legs and breast of the chicken and cut the rest into very small pieces. Make pilâv with three quarters of the chicken stock but before adding the rice to the boiling stock put in the pieces of cut up chicken, bring to the boil again and then put in the rice. Now proceed as for the making of plain pilâv (page 115).

In a separate pan melt 15g (½oz) of the butter, add the flour and cook for 3 minutes, stirring all the time. Add the remaining chicken stock, stir, add the cream gradually and stir until smooth and creamy, about 5 minutes. Remove from the heat, add the rest of the butter, stir and keep hot.

Serve the pilâv, arrange the legs and slices of breast of chicken around the dish, pour on the cream sauce and sprinkle with the grated Parmesan cheese.

Serve immediately.

Turkish cooking

Pilaw With Lamb

Kuzulu Pilâv

450g (1lb) lamb
450ml (¾ pint) chicken stock
1 teaspoon white pepper
1 onion, chopped
1 teaspoon cinnamon
50g (2oz) butter
1 tablespoon currants
1 tomato, skinned and chopped
3 sprigs parsley

225g (8oz) long-grain rice
1 tablespoon pine kernels
1 teaspoon sugar
1 tablespoon chopped fresh dill
50ml (2floz) vegetable oil
225g (8oz) lamb's liver
½ teaspoon salt
3 spring onions
1 leaf rosemary

Put the lamb and the vegetable oil into a baking tin and roast at 190°C/375°F/Gas 5 until nicely browned, basting every 10 minutes. Remove when cooked and keep in a warm place.

Clean the liver and cut into very small pieces, sauté for 3 minutes in half the butter, then leave aside to keep warm. Cut up the spring onions and sauté in the same butter for 2 minutes and leave aside to keep warm.

Clean and prepare the rice as for plain pilâv (page 115). Melt the remaining butter and fry the onions until they begin to brown slightly. Add the pine kernels and cook until these are golden brown, be careful that the onions do not burn during this time. Add the rice and fry for another 5 minutes. Add the pepper, salt, cleaned currants, sugar, spring onions, herbs, tomatoes and stock. Stir once, cover and cook for 5 minutes on a high heat then reduce the heat to very low and cook until all the liquid has been absorbed by the rice, about 6 minutes more, although if the rice is old it may take a minute or so longer. Add the liver and the minced parsley, stir with a wooden spoon, add the spring onions, cover with a napkin and put on the lid. Leave to 'rest' for 40 minutes as near to the heat as possible. Stir once more then serve with slices of roast lamb on top garnished with cinnamon.

Borek and Pilaw
Pilâv ve Börekler

Plain Pilaw

Pilâv

225g (8oz) long-grain rice
25g (1oz) butter

450ml (¾ pint) chicken stock
½ teaspoon salt

Clean the rice, lay on a shallow dish and pour boiling water over it. Leave until the water is quite cold, strain and wash several times under running cold water.

Melt the butter in a large pan, heat but do not allow to burn. Add the stock and salt and bring to the boil quickly. Add the drained rice and cook at the same temperature for 5 minutes, then turn down the heat to very, very low and cook until all the stock has been absorbed, 7–8 minutes, when there should be holes all over the rice. Test with a wooden spoon and if this stands upright then the rice is cooked.

Remove from the heat, take off the lid, put a napkin over the saucepan then replace the lid again. Leave close to the heat to keep hot for 30–35 minutes. This 'resting' period is the most important part of pilâv making.

Remove the lid and napkin, stir well with a wooden spoon until each grain stands separately and serve at once.

Note: For the most flavoursome results use Basmati or Patna rice. A light tossing before cooking in melted butter or olive oil helps improve separation. For a neutral base, substitute spring water for chicken stock. To make Almond, Saffron, Spring or Tomato Pilâv, supplement respectively with ground and finely chopped blanched almonds, saffron, spring onions and chives, or puréed tomatoes, varying the amount of each according to taste. For Oriental Pilâv add sultanas, currants, pine kernels and fresh peas, together with slivers of red pepper or pimento as desired. (AO)

Turkish cooking

Shrimp Pilaw With Saffron

Teke ve Safronli Pilâv

225g (8oz) long-grain rice
25g (1oz) butter
1 carrot, diced
1 clove of garlic, mashed
3 peppercorns
600ml (1 pint) water

225g (8oz) cooked shrimps
2 stalks celery, cut small
1 large onion, chopped
½ teaspoon salt
1 teaspoon chopped fresh basil
½ teaspoon saffron

Melt the butter and fry in it the onions, garlic, celery and carrot, until the onions are a golden brown. Add half the shrimps, the peppercorns and all the herbs and cook for another 3–4 minutes. Add the water and cook for another 15 minutes. Remove the peppercorns and pass the rest of the mixture through a sieve. Dissolve the saffron in a very little hot water then pour into the liquid through muslin.

From this liquid, measure out 450ml (¾ pint), add a quarter of the butter, allow to melt then add the washed and cleaned rice. After 2 minutes' cooking turn the heat down to very low and cook for 15 minutes, when all the liquid should be absorbed by the rice. Put the rest of the shrimps on top of the rice, cover again and leave to 'rest' for 40 minutes with a napkin under the lid to absorb the excess moisture.

Stir once to separate the grains and serve immediately.

Stuffing No. 2 For Green Peppers, Tomatoes, Vine Leaves etc

225g (8oz) long-grain rice
125ml (4floz) water
5 large onions, chopped finely
1 tablespoon pine kernels
1 teaspoon sugar
1 teaspoon mixed herbs
Chopped sprig of fresh mint

225ml (8floz) olive oil
125ml (4floz) cider
1 large tomato, skinned
1 tablespoon currants
1 teaspoon pepper
Chopped sprig of fresh dill
Salt

Clean and cover the rice with hot water and leave aside until the water is cold. Wash several times under running water, strain and leave aside.

Fry the onions in the oil for 10 minutes. Add the rice and pine kernels, cover the pan and cook for 20 minutes on a moderate heat, stirring occasionally to avoid sticking. Add the chopped tomato, currants, dill, mint, mixed herbs, water and cider, stir and cook for another 15 minutes. Add the sugar last of all and use the stuffing as directed in the recipes.

Note: This stuffing must only be used in dishes which are to be served cold.

Turkish cooking

Desserts
Tatlilar

Almond Cream With Sherry Sauce

Sarapli Kremli Badem

50g (2oz) butter
50g (2oz) ground sweet almonds
4 large egg yolks
50g (2oz) caster sugar

50g (2oz) grated chocolate,
  unsweetened
4 egg whites

Brush a tube mould with almond oil.

Cream the butter and sugar until white and fluffy then beat in the egg yolks, one at a time, and continue beating for 2 minutes.

Whisk the egg whites until they hold a peak, then fold gently into the mixture.

Add the ground almonds and chocolate and stir once, thoroughly but quickly. Pour the mixture into the mould and steam over hot water for 45 minautes.

Sherry Sauce:

100g (4oz) sugar
225ml (8floz) dark sherry

100g (4oz) grated chocolate,
  unsweetened

Put the sugar, salt, chocolate and sherry into a pan and cook until thick, stirring all the time.

When the almond cream is unmoulded pour the hot sauce over it, first having filled the centre of the mould with vanilla ice cream.

Turkish cooking

Almond Fingers

Badem Tatlisi

100g (4oz) ground sweet almonds
6 large eggs
900g (2lb) sugar
600ml (1 pint) fresh peach juice
Halved fresh peaches

100g (4oz) plain flour
25g (1oz) butter
⅛ teaspoon salt
50g (2oz) pralined almonds

Grease and flour a 22.5cm (9in) square tin.

Separate the egg yolks, add just under 225g (8oz) sugar and beat for 6–7 minutes.

Add the salt to the egg whites and beat until stiff and glossy, then fold carefully into the yolks. Add the almonds and the flour and the melted butter. Stir quickly and pour into the greased tin. Bake for 50 minutes at 190°C/375°F/Gas 5.

Put the peach juice and the remaining sugar into a saucepan and boil for 15 minutes uncovered, stirring until all the sugar has been dissolved. Pour this syrup over the almond sweet (it should be left in the tin until cold) and leave aside overnight if possible.

Cut into fingers and serve with the halved peaches and pralined almonds.

Note: To praline almonds: Chop some almonds and brown them very evenly in the oven, sprinkling them frequently with icing sugar. The heat of the oven causes the sugar to caramelise on the almonds.

Almond Tart with Caramel Sauce

Karemela Salçali Badem Tatlisi

6 egg yolks	75g (3oz) plain flour, sifted four times
1 teaspoon baking powder	6 egg whites
1 teaspoon salt	175g (6oz) toasted almonds, finely chopped
½ teaspoon cream of tartar	
225g (8oz) sugar	Hot water
Whipped cream filling (almond flavour)	Caramel sauce

Caramelise three quarters of the sugar by melting it in a heavy saucepan over a low heat, stirring continuously until brown. Add the hot water and stir until the mixture is very smooth and creamy.

Beat the egg yolks until thick and lemon coloured and stir in two tablespoons of the slightly cooled caramel mixture. Sift together the flour, baking powder and salt and stir into the egg yolks.

Beat the egg whites and cream of tartar together until the mixture holds a peak, then beat in gradually the rest of the sugar and go on beating until very stiff and glossy. Fold in the toasted almonds and last of all fold in the egg yolk mixture.

Line two 22.5cm (9in) sandwich tins with greased paper, brushed over with a little warm almond oil, and pour in the mixture. Bake at 190°C/375°F/Gas 5 for about 30 minutes or until, when touched gently with the finger, no imprint remains.

Turn out of the pans, remove the paper and cool. Put together with almond flavoured whipped cream filling and cover with caramel sauce, which is made as follows. Add to the caramelised sugar left in the heavy saucepan:

100g (9oz) sugar	50g (2oz) butter
¼ teaspoon salt	175ml (6floz) single cream

Stir together until smooth and cook over a moderate heat, stirring now and then until the mixture reaches boiling point. Remove from the heat. When partly cooled (do not stir during this time) pour over the top and sides of the tart. Serve cold.

To Make Whipped Cream Filling:

½ teaspoon gelatin	1 tablespoon single cream
225ml (8floz) double cream	50g (2oz) sifted icing sugar
1 teaspoon almond essence	

Soften the gelatin in the single cream then dissolve over a pan of hot water. Whip the double cream until stiff, beat in the icing sugar, the cooled gelatin and the almond flavouring. Chill slightly before use.

Apricot Meringue

Kayisi

450g (1lb) fresh apricots
100g (4oz) ground sweet almonds
150ml (¼ pint) whipped cream
¾ teaspoon cream of tartar
3–4 tablespoons dark sherry

350g (12oz) sugar
50g (2oz) pine kernels
3 egg whites
1 tablespoon lemon juice

Put the stoned apricots and lemon juice into a saucepan and cook on a low heat until plenty of the liquid has been extracted from the fruit. Add two thirds of the sugar, stir until dissolved, cover and cook for 30 minutes over a low heat. Remove from the heat and cool.

Mix half of the ground almonds with the rest of the sugar and the pine kernels with enough sherry to make a softish paste. Fill the apricots with this mixture. Arrange in a greased glass oven dish, sprinkling the rest of the ground almonds over them and adding their own syrup.

Beat the egg whites with the cream of tartar until stiff and glossy and spread over the whole, taking special care that the meringue reaches right to the sides of the dish and the apricots are not exposed in any place. Bake at 150°C/300°F/Gas 2 until the meringue is firm and set and delicately browned.

Serve hot.

Turkish cooking

Ashurey

Asure

100g (4oz) wheat or branflakes
225g (8oz) sugar
50g (2oz) haricot beans, cooked
100g (4oz) dates
75g (3oz) figs
50g (2oz) blanched almonds, halved
125ml (4floz) rosewater
Pomegranate(s)

450ml (¾ pint) milk
50g (2oz) long-grain rice
50g (2oz) butter beans, cooked
50g (2oz) currants
100g (4oz) sultanas
50g (2oz) chopped walnuts
25g (1oz) pine kernels

The haricot and butter beans should be soaked overnight, then cooked until soft but unbroken, drained and left to cool.

Cook the wheat and rice in separate saucepans in plenty of water until they are very tender. Strain, keeping the water in which they were cooked, and put through a sieve.

Using 1.2 litres (2 pints) of the water used for cooking the rice and wheat, add the milk and sugar and bring to the boil, stirring until the sugar is dissolved. Boil until it thickens, a few minutes, then add the beans and all the other ingredients. Boil for a further 2–3 minutes.

Serve cold in individual cups decorated with sultanas, whole walnuts and segments of pomegranate drenched in icing sugar.

Baklava With Walnuts

Baklava

Baklava or filo pastry
100g (4oz) butter
225ml (8floz) water

100g (4oz) finely chopped walnuts
350g (12oz) sugar
1 tablespoon lemon juice

Making baklava pastry is an art and it cannot be made at home. Even in the Middle East, where the women spend most of their time in the kitchen, baklava pastry is bought from the market. There are many recipes for the homemade product but baklava made with them never achieves the same lightness as the market product.

Grease and flour a shallow 22.5cm (9in) square tin.

Roll out the baklava pastry very carefully to avoid breaking and cut into eight pieces which should fit the pan exactly.

Take four pieces of the pastry and brush each thoroughly with melted butter and lay them in the tin one on top of the other. Cover the fourth layer with chopped walnuts. Place the other four pieces of pastry on top of the first four (again each layer brushed thoroughly with the melted butter) and if there is any butter left pour it on the top layer. With a very sharp knife cut right through the eight layers in diamond shapes. Bake at 190°C/375°F/Gas 5 until nicely browned, just over 1 hour.

Put the sugar, water and lemon juice in a pan and boil for 15 minutes, stirring until the sugar is dissolved. Cool a little.

When the baklava is taken from the oven, brush the whole top with butter and leave for 10 minutes. Pour the syrup into the tin and allow to cool. Serve after 24 hours' rest.

Turkish cooking

Baklava With Ground Almonds

Bademli Baklava

Baklava or filo pastry
350g (12oz) butter
225ml (8floz) fresh apricot juice
Halved fresh apricots

225g (8oz) ground sweet almonds
350g (12oz) sugar
½ tablespoon lemon juice

Grease a shallow 22.5cm (9in) square tray.

Use the pastry as in the previous recipe and cut into eight pieces the size of the tray.

Line the pan with a piece of the pastry, brush thoroughly over every part with melted butter and spread evenly with ground almonds. Continue like this until the eight pieces of the pastry have been used, finishing off with a layer of plain pastry. Use up any leftover butter on this. Cut with a very sharp knife through the eight pieces, in squares, and bake at 190°C/375°F/Gas 5 for just over an hour until brown.

Make a syrup with the apricot juice, lemon and sugar and boil for 15 minutes.

Brush the cooked baklava with butter and leave for 10 minutes then pour the warm syrup over them.

Leave for 24 hours before serving with halved fresh apricots rolled in icing sugar.

Blackcurrant Sponge

Kusüzümü Tatlisi

1 tablespoon gelatin	50ml (2floz) cold water
225ml (8floz) hot blackcurrant juice	175g (6oz) brown sugar
2 tablespoons lemon juice	2 egg whites
50g (2oz) fresh blackcurrants	150ml (¼ pint) whipped cream

Soften the gelatin in the cold water. Stir in the hot juice, lemon juice, and sugar and stir until all the sugar has dissolved. Strain and cool, stirring now and then. When partly set, whisk with an electric hand whisk until frothy. Beat the egg whites until they hold a point and fold in, then beat again until all the mixture is stiff and holds a point.

Pile into tall glasses, chill for several hours and serve with whipped cream and fresh blackcurrants.

Turkish cooking

Chicken Breasts

Tavuk Gögüs

½ chicken breast, uncooked
225ml (8floz) single cream
2 tablespoons cornflour
⅛ teaspoon salt
Enough dry white wine to cover the
   chicken when cooking

600ml (1 pint) milk
225g (8oz) sugar
40g (1½oz) ground rice
1 teaspoon ground cinnamon
Crystallised violets

Cook the chicken breast in the wine slowly, removing from the heat a few minutes before thoroughly cooked. Strain off the wine and shred the breast finely. Put the shreds into boiling water to cleanse away any fatty residue and wash well. Repeat this process several times with fresh hot water, then dry and leave aside. Put the milk, cream, salt and sugar in a saucepan and bring to the boil, stirring frequently to prevent the cream from sticking. Mix the cornflour and ground rice with a little cold water and add to the boiling milk and cook until the mixture is of a fairly thick consistency, stirring continuously. Add the shredded chicken breast and cook for another 7–8 minutes. Pour into individual moulds, wetted, and chill thoroughly.

   Unmould, sprinkle with cinnamon and decorate with the crystallised violets.

Note: The wine in which the breast was stewed can be used in soups or stocks, etc.

Chocolate Marshmallow

Çikolata Tatlisi

1 tablespoon gelatin
450ml (¾ pint) milk
50g (2oz) unsweetened chocolate
25g (1oz) ground sweet almonds
150ml (¼ pint) whipped cream

50ml (2floz) milk
100g (4oz) sugar
100g (4oz) chopped marshmallows
3 egg whites
Slivers of milk chocolate

Dissolve the gelatin in 50ml (2floz) of milk.

Put the 450ml (¾ pint) of milk, sugar and unsweetened chocolate into a saucepan and heat. Beat very fast for 2 minutes, then remove from the heat. Add the gelatin and milk and continue beating until smooth and creamy. Remove from the heat and chill until it begins to set.

Stir in the marshmallows and the almonds and fold in the egg whites, stiffly beaten. Fold in the whipped cream and chill thoroughly.

Serve in tall glasses decorated with slivers of milk chocolate.

Turkish cooking

Fruit Compôte

Meyva Kompostosu

175g (6oz) strawberries
175g (6oz) green grapes, seedless
1½ tablespoons gelatin
450ml (¾ pint) unsweetened grape juice, hot
⅛ teaspoon salt
1 teaspoon grated lemon rind

Whipped cream (Cointreau flavoured)
175g (6oz) black cherries, stoned
175g (6oz) halved fresh peaches
50ml (2floz) cold water
175g (6oz) caster sugar
1 teaspoon lemon juice
50ml (2floz) Cointreau

Soften the gelatin in cold water, stir in the hot grape juice, sugar and salt. Stir until the sugar and gelatin are completely dissolved. Cool. Stir in the lemon juice and rind and chill until it starts to set. Add the Cointreau and whisk well. Add the fruits and pour into an oiled mould. Chill until set.

Unmould and serve with whipped cream.

Note: Mass-produced propreity brands of rose water are not usually as subtle in taste or as delicately perfumed as the Indian or Persian natural varieties. (AO)

Ground Rice Pudding

Muhallebi

600ml (1 pint) milk
175g (6oz) caster sugar
40g (1½oz) ground rice
⅛ teaspoon salt
A little icing sugar

225ml (8floz) single cream
1½ tablespoons cornflour
50g (2oz) ground sweet almonds
125ml (4floz) rosewater, triple
    strength
Crystallised roses for garnish

Boil the milk and cream with the sugar and salt.

Mix the cornflour and ground rice with a little water and add this slowly to the boiling milk, stirring continuously. Cook until the mixture becomes a thickish custard (stirring all the time as this sweet burns easily). Add the ground almonds, stir and remove from the heat.

Pour into individual moulds (wetted) and chill.

Unmould, sprinkle each with rosewater and a little icing sugar and decorate with the roses.

Note: Mass-produced propriety brands of rose water are not usually as subtle in taste or as delicately perfumed as the Indian or Persian natural varieties. (AO)

Turkish cooking

Helva

225g (8oz) fine semolina
225ml (8floz) milk
100g (4oz) butter
½ teaspoon vanilla essence

225g (8oz) sugar
225ml (8floz) single cream
25g (1oz) blanched almonds, halved

Melt the butter and add the almonds and cook for 2 minutes. Add the semolina and continue cooking over a gentle heat for 40 minutes, stirring continuously.

In a saucepan boil the milk and the cream and add sugar. Remove from the heat and add the vanilla essence.

Add the milk and cream to the semolina mixture, stir well, cover and leave near the heat for 15–20 minutes.

Serve when only slightly warm.

Note: The time of 40 minutes given above for the cooking of the semolina is correct only if the correct heat is used, it may take a few minutes longer or less, but the surest guide is when the almonds have browned considerably and a definite almond smell comes from the mixture.

Kadingöbegi

225g (8oz) flour
450g (1lb) sugar
450ml (¾ pint) water
3 eggs
225g (8oz) butter, for frying

40g (1½oz) butter
450ml (¾ pint) water
½ tablespoon lemon juice
⅛ teaspoon salt
90ml (3floz) whipped cream

Put the sugar, lemon juice and 450ml (¾ pint) of water in a saucepan, boil for 15 minutes then leave aside to cool.

Melt 40g (1½ oz) butter and when sizzling add the salt and the rest of the water. Bring to the boil and add the flour. Cook for 5 minutes, stirring all the time. Remove from the heat and when cold add the eggs and knead for 7–8 minutes. Take pieces of the dough, about the size of a walnut, and shape into balls. Flatten and make a hole through the centre with your finger, grease round the hole with a very little almond oil.

Melt the butter and fry the balls, at first on a very low heat until they start to swell when the heat should be slightly raised. Cook on both sides until a deep golden brown. Toss each one into the syrup, leave for 5 minutes and serve cold with the whipped cream.

Always remember to cool off the butter before starting to cook another batch and to increase the heat only when the balls begin swelling.

Turkish cooking

Keskül

225g (8oz) sugar
450ml (¾ pint) single cream
100g (4oz) ground sweet almonds
75g (3oz) pomegranate
25g (1oz) pine kernels

450ml (¾ pint) milk
25g (1oz) ground rice
50g (2oz) grated fresh coconut
⅛ teaspoon salt
150ml (¼ pint) clotted cream

Pour half of the scalded cream over half of the ground almonds, stir well, pass through a sieve and then put aside.

Boil the rest of the cream with the milk, add salt, and stir frequently as cream sticks very quickly. Mix the ground rice with a little milk and pour into the saucepan. Boil gently for 5 minutes, stirring all the time. Add the sugar and the sieved cream and almond mixture and boil until thick. Remove from the heat and pour into a wetted tube mould. Chill for several hours.

Unmould and fill the centre with the rest of the ground almonds, mixed with the grated coconut and pine kernels and top with the pomegranate.

Sprinkle with icing sugar and finish off with clotted cream.

Lemon Pudding

Limonlu Krema

25g (1oz) sifted plain flour
¼ teaspoon salt
90ml (3floz) lemon juice
225ml (8floz) single cream
300ml (½ pint) set lemon jelly

225g (8oz) caster sugar
Rind of 1 lemon, grated
3 large egg yolks
3 egg whites
100g (4oz) vanilla ice cream

Sift together the flour, sugar and salt. Stir in the lemon rind and juice. Beat the egg yolks until thick and creamy, then stir into the mixture and add the cream.

Beat the egg whites until they hold a peak, then fold in. Pour into a greased ring mould, set in a pan of water and bake at 190°C/375°F/Gas 5 for 55–60 minutes.

Allow to cool thoroughly.

After unmoulding, fill the centre of the ring with chopped lemon jelly and serve with vanilla ice cream.

Turkish cooking

Lemon Jelly

Jelatinli Limon

1½ tablespoons gelatin
50ml (2floz) lemon juice
Rind of 1 lemon

225ml (8floz) hot water
50ml (2floz) dry white wine, hot
100g (4oz) caster sugar

Dissolve the gelatin in the lemon juice, add the sugar, hot water and lemon rind and stir until the sugar has dissolved. Strain through muslin, add the hot wine and pour into a wetted mould. Leave to set.

Lokma

450g (1lb) plain flour	225g (8oz) soft butter, for frying
1 tablespoon yeast	350g (12oz) sugar
15g (½oz) butter	½ teaspoon salt
300ml (½ pint) dry white wine	175ml (6floz) water
90ml (3floz) whipped cream	100g (4oz) fresh pineapple slices

Put the wine and sugar into a saucepan and when the sugar has dissolved bring to the boil, stirring all the time, and boil rapidly without a lid for 15 minutes. Remove from the heat and allow to cool.

Sieve the flour three times, add the yeast, dissolved in 1 tablespoon of water, 15g (½oz) of butter and the salt. Add the water slowly and mix into a thick batter. Leave in a warm place to rise for 1 hour. Punch down, cover and leave to rise again for a further 1 hour. Now put the batter through a forcing bag and pipe pieces the size of a walnut into the butter for frying, which should by this time be very hot. Fry until pale brown and remove from the heat. After 15 minutes has elapsed return the pieces again to the hot butter and cook until a deep golden brown. Toss in the cooled syrup, leave for 5 minutes then remove to a serving dish.

Serve cold with the whipped cream and pineapple slices.

Turkish cooking

Plum Desserts

Erik Tatlisi

450g (1lb) large black plums
150g (50oz) sifted plain flour
2 teaspoons caster sugar
50g (2oz) ground sweet almonds
225–350g (8–12oz) butter
Chopped pistachio nuts

125ml (4floz) Marsala
2 egg whites
1½ teaspoons grated lemon rind
A little rosewater (about 3
    tablespoons)
Icing sugar
90ml (4floz) whipped cream

Wash the plums and stone them. Do this with a long needle, taking care not to break the outer skin. Fill with ground sweet almonds sprinkled with a little rosewater.

Whisk the Marsala, flour, lemon rind and sugar together to make a sort of batter and leave aside for 1 hour. Whisk again and fold in the stiffly-beaten egg whites.

Melt the butter, coat the plums in the wine batter, and fry until a golden brown (the batter should puff up considerably).

Drain and roll in icing sugar and pistachio nuts. Serve hot with a little whipped cream piped over each.

Raspberry Shortcake

Frambuvaz Kurabiyesi

225g (8oz) sifted plain flour
2½ teaspoons baking powder
75g (3oz) soft butter
450g (1lb) raspberries
50ml (2floz) port
40g (1½oz) plain flour
225ml (8floz) water

40g (1½oz) caster sugar
1 teaspoon salt
150ml (¼ pint) milk
100g (4oz) caster sugar
50g (2oz) soft butter
350g (12oz) sugar

Marinate the raspberries, port and 100g (4oz) of caster sugar for 1 hour, turning the fruit now and then.

Put 350g (12oz) of sugar and the water in an oblong baking pan and boil for 6 minutes, stirring all the time.

Sift together 225g (8oz) of flour, 40g (1½oz) of caster sugar, the baking powder and the salt and blend in 75g (3oz) of softened butter, then stir in the milk. Knead lightly and roll out to 8mm (⅛in) thick and into an oblong shape 15x30cm (6x12in).

Spread this with the marinated raspberries, using the liquid as well.

Mix 50g (2oz) of soft butter and 40g (1½oz) of flour and spread over the fruit. Roll up lengthways, seal the edges carefully and place the roll in the hot syrup in the baking pan.

Bake for 35–40 minutes at 230°C/450°F/Gas 8, basting with the syrup from time to time.

Serve cold cut into thick slices with whole raspberries and unsweetened whipped cream.

Turkish cooking

Revani

225g (8oz) fine semolina
8 eggs
25g (1oz) plain flour
2 teaspoons lemon rind
100g (4oz) clotted cream

900g (2lb) sugar
25g (1oz) butter
600ml (1 pint) Marsala
⅛ teaspoon salt

Grease and flour a 22.5cm (9in) square tin.

Separate the yolks of the eggs, add a quarter of the sugar and the lemon rind and beat for 7–8 minutes.

Beat the whites with the salt until they hold a peak and fold into the yolks. Add the sifted flour and the semolina, stir very carefully then pour in the butter which should have been melted. Pour into the greased tin and cook at 190°C/375°F/Gas 5 until delicately browned, about 1 hour.

Put the Marsala and the remaining sugar into a saucepan, bring to the boil slowly, stirring until all the sugar has been dissolved. Boil rapidly for 15 minutes, uncovered.

Pour the hot syrup over the revani, in the tin in which it was cooked, and leave to cool.

Serve after 24 hours with clotted cream.

Rice in Wine Syrup

Sütlâç Sarapli

100g (4oz) long-grain rice	225ml (8floz) milk
225ml (8floz) single cream	40g (1½oz) caster sugar
25g (1oz) butter	2 large eggs
⅛ teaspoon salt	40g (1½oz) seedless raisins
25g (1oz) ground sweet almonds	150ml (¼ pint) whipped cream
175g (6oz) sugar	90ml (3floz) red or white wine

Clean the rice and boil it in plenty of water until soft. Strain off any surplus water and add the milk, cream, butter, raisins, caster sugar and salt. Cook until the mixture is very thick, stirring frequently to prevent sticking. Remove from the heat and allow to get cold.

Add the beaten eggs and the almonds and stir well. Pour into a greased baking dish and bake until the top is golden brown at 190°C/375°F/Gas 5. Remove from the oven, cut into triangular shapes in the baking dish and leave to cool.

Put 175g (6oz) of sugar and the wine into a saucepan and boil until a thickish syrup is obtained, about 10 minutes fast boiling, stirring until all the sugar has been dissolved.

Pour this over the rice shapes and serve cold, any syrup not absorbed by the rice can be poured over, with whipped cream.

Turkish cooking

Strawberry Cream Puffs

Çilekli Pastalar

225ml (8floz) water
100g (4oz) sifted plain flour
300ml (½ pint) double cream
175g (6oz) chopped strawberries

100g (4oz) butter
4 large eggs
100g (4oz) icing sugar

Heat the water and the butter to boiling point. Add the flour and stir constantly until the mixture leaves the sides of the pan and forms a ball (about 1½–2 minutes).

Remove from the heat and cool.

Beat in the eggs one by one and continue beating until the mixture is smooth and velvety. Drop the mixture from a large spoon onto an ungreased baking tray, at least 7.5cm (3in) apart, and bake at 190°C/375°F/Gas 5 for about 45 minutes or until they are puffed, dry and golden brown. Cool slowly in a warm, draught free place.

Cut off the tops with a sharp knife and scoop out any soft dough inside. Whip the cream until it is very stiff, add the icing sugar and beat again. Fold in the strawberries and fill the puffs with this mixture. Replace the tops and dust with icing sugar. Serve cold.

Tulumba Tatlisi

25g (1oz) butter
15g (½oz) ground rice
3 large eggs
225ml (8floz) olive oil
225ml (8floz) white grape juice
Bananas cut lengthways

100g (4oz) plain flour
7g (¼oz) arrowroot
⅛ teaspoon salt
350g (12oz) sugar
125ml (4floz) dry white wine

Boil the sugar and grape juice for 15 minutes until a thickish syrup has formed, then remove from the heat and put aside.

Melt the butter and add the wine and salt. Bring to boiling point slowly. Add the twice sifted flour very gradually and cook over a low heat for 8 minutes, stirring all the time. Remove from the heat and add the ground rice and arrowroot (previously mixed with a little water). Leave to cool.

When almost cold add the eggs and knead for 8 minutes, then put through a forcing bag with an 8mm (⅓in) wide nozzle.

Heat the olive oil a little and pipe 5cm (2in) lengths of the mixture into it. Cook on a low heat until they begin to swell, then increase the heat and cook until they are golden brown on both sides. (If more than one batch has to be cooked, always cool off the olive oil before piping the fresh mixture into it and never increase the heat until the swelling has started.) Toss the tulumba in the syrup, leave for 5 minutes and serve cold on the sliced bananas.

Turkish cooking

Turkish Delight

Lokum

900g (2lb) sugar
500g (2oz) cornflour
1 teaspoon almond oil
2 teaspoons rosewater
A few drops of red food colouring

450ml (¾ pint) water
1 teaspoon cream of tartar
150g (5oz) icing sugar
1 tablespoon finely chopped
   pistachio nuts
90ml (3floz) white grape juice

Boil the sugar and water for 20 minutes, stirring until the sugar has dissolved. Mix the cornflour with the grape juice and add this, gradually, to the syrup, stirring all the time. Add the cream of tartar and continue stirring. Boil until the mixture is thick and no smell of cornflour comes from it, then remove from the heat. Add the rosewater and the food colouring and pour into a long shallow tray well-brushed with almond oil and leave until cold. With a sharp knife cut into squares, roll in icing sugar and serve.

   The sweets can also be rolled in a mixture of half icing sugar and half coconut.

Turkish Coffee

Kahve

To each *small* coffee cup use 2 teaspoons Turkish coffee (this is the fine, powdered coffee, as fine as cocoa) and from 1–2 teaspoons sugar, depending upon how sweet you like it.

A brass, copper-lined cezva with a long handle is the correct implement for cooking it, preferably over a charcoal fire. But a small saucepan may be used quite successfully.

For three people use:

3 coffee cups cold water (the smallest coffee cups)
3–6 heaped teaspoons sugar
6 rounded teaspoons Turkish coffee

Put the water, sugar and coffee into the saucepan and over a very low heat (this is most important), bring to the boil, stirring at first until all the sugar has been dissolved. Allow to come barely to the boil, then remove from the heat and allow the froth to subside. Repeat this three times, allow to subside and serve immediately, pouring a little into each cup at first so that the brown froth is distributed evenly.

Incidentally, never wash the saucepan too thoroughly. Keep one saucepan for the making of Turkish coffee and never do more than rinse it out in cold water. In this way the saucepan becomes well and truly 'seasoned' and your coffee flavour improves.

Turkish cooking

Index

Turkish cooking